International Studies

vol. 5

CLEMSON
UNIVERSITY
PRESS

CONTENTS

Volume 5, Issue 1

SPECIAL ISSUE: *WHEELS AND BUTTERFLIES*

Margaret Mills Harper
    Introduction to the Introductions: *Wheels and Butterflies* as Comedy   1

Charles I. Armstrong
    Cornered: Intimate Relations in *The Words upon the Window-Pane*   10

Inés Bigot
    The 'endless dance of contrapuntal energy': Conflict and Disunity
    in *Fighting the Waves*   26

Alexandra Poulain
    '[...] but a play': Laughter and the Reinvention of Theater in
    The Resurrection   40

Akiko Manabe
    'Are you that flighty?' 'I am that flighty.': *The Cat and the Moon*
    and *Kyogen* Revisited   52

REVIEWS

Lloyd (Meadhbh) Houston
    Science, Technology, and Irish Modernism, edited by
    Kathryn Conrad, Cóilín Parsons, and Julie McCormick Weng   70

Claire Nally
    A Reader's Guide to Yeats's A Vision, by Neil Mann   78

Maria Rita Drumond Viana
    The Collected Letters of W. B. Yeats Volume V: 1908–1910, edited by
    John Kelly and Ronald Schuchard   82

Zsuzanna Balázs
    Precarious Bodies and Physical Theater: A Review of DancePlayers'
    The Dreaming of the Bones by W. B. Yeats   87

Notes on Contributors   98

INTRODUCTION TO THE INTRODUCTIONS:
WHEELS AND BUTTERFLIES AS COMEDY

Margaret Mills Harper

On August 24, 1929, Yeats wrote to his old friend Olivia Shakespear about his excitement at the public reception of his play *Fighting the Waves*. It was, he told her, "my greatest success on the stage since Kathleen-ni-Houlihan, & its production was a great event here, the politicians & the governor general & the American Minister present" (*CL InteLex* 5277). The play was a prose rewriting of *The Only Jealousy of Emer*, published ten years earlier. Not only had Yeats replaced poetry with prose and simplified the action, making it easier for an audience to follow, but the Abbey production was also enhanced by the striking modernist masks of the Dutch sculptor Hildo Krop, music by the bad boy futurist composer George Antheill, and the dance of Ninette de Valois, perhaps the most influential dancer/choreographer of her generation. The work, joining as it did words, music, movement, and visual art into what Yeats called "a new form," thrilled him. Still, he told Shakespear:

> I regretted as I often do when we are more than usually spirited at the Abbey, that [you] could not be here. One writes & works for one['s] friends, & those who read, or at any rate those who listen are people about whom one cares nothing—that seems the general rule at any rate (CL InteLex 5277).

This observation, that one "writes & works for one's friends" but that the main audience or readership is comprised of people "about whom one cares nothing," is the idea that grinds and flitters into and through *Wheels and Butterflies*, published by Macmillan in London in 1934 and New York the following year. This book does not get a lot of discussion. On the surface, it seems a somewhat makeshift affair, comprised of four late plays and four long, cantankerous, and often seemingly irrelevant introductions to them. All the plays were published elsewhere, and when they were composed Yeats was under obligation not to publish new books while the ultimately doomed Edition de Luxe was in preparation. He argued for publishing *Wheels and Butterflies* (perhaps chafing at the repeated delays for the de Luxe edition) by claiming that the new introductions weren't available elsewhere and were "rather long commentaries on the plays, not mere notes but general criticisms" (*CL InteLex* 5418, letter to Hansard Watt, December 12, 1930). The contents of *Wheels and Butterflies* could later be added to the de Luxe volume to be called *Plays and Controversies*, Yeats noted, in the midst of very practical negotiations with his publisher through his agent.

The commentaries *are* long. In total, out of the 163 pages of the volume, about a third (forty-nine pages) are taken up with the introductions. Antheil's music is printed at the back, and if those pages are included in the count, the plays themselves make up less than half of the collected material. This large percentage of seemingly peripheral matter is reminiscent of *A Vision*, which leads a reader through large quantities of seemingly ancillary components before arriving at the explicit exposition of the system in the main body of the book.

The title, *Wheels and Butterflies*, alludes to the same antinomy of the projected but unmaterialized title *Plays and Controversies*. The plays are the butterflies, offering art rather than politics, aimless joy (which Yeats often described using the image of a butterfly) rather than driving rhetoric. The introductions are the wheels, inexorable and perhaps making less real progress in their circular motion than a butterfly's erratic flight path. In another letter to Shakespear, Yeats described the general idea:

> I want to bring out a book of four plays called "My Wheels & Butterflies"—the wheels are the four introductions. Dublin is said to be full of little societies meeting in cellars & garrets so I shall put this rhyme on a fly-leaf
>
> To cellar & garret
> A wheel I send
> But every butterfly
> To a friend.
> The "Wheels" are addressed to Ireland mainly—a scheme of intellectual nationalism (*CL InteLex* 5414, December 2, 1930).

The first introduction in the collection, to the play *The Words upon the Window-Pane*, defines the terms:

> Somebody said the other night that Dublin was full of clubs—he himself knew four—that met in cellars and garrets and had for their object our general improvement. He was scornful, said that they had all begun by drawing up a programme and passing a resolution against the censorship and would never do anything else. When I began my public life Dublin was full of such clubs that passed resolutions and drew up programmes, and though the majority did nothing else some helped to find an audience for a school of writers (*W&B* 5, *VPl* 957).[1]

"Our" general improvement refers to Ireland, though Yeats makes sure to note that the former nationalist era and the current situation, well after the establishment of the Free State, are two versions of some general principle: "Political failure and political success have had the same result" (*W&B* 5, *VPl* 957).

In this special issue Charles I. Armstrong, Inés Bigot, Alexandra Poulain, and Akiko Manabe discuss the volume's four plays: *The Words upon the Window-Pane*, *Fighting the Waves*, *The Resurrection*, and *The Cat and the Moon*. Their essays are the butterflies, if you like, analyzing creative texts. My contribution serves as an introduction to their work and offers some discussion of Yeats's strange introductory essays. Thus, this introduction in relation to the essays that follow parallels Yeats's: it is the wheels, squeaking with strain rather than fluttering in scholarly joy. My hope is that these wheels, like Yeats's, may provide a quirky counterweight with a part to play in the larger drama.

A live question for *Wheels and Butterflies* concerns its readership. The consumer of the volume would presumably fall into one of the two categories defined in the epigraph: "To Garret or Cellar a wheel I send, / But every butterfly to a friend." Given that Garret and Cellar are synecdoches for earnest and narrow-minded improvers who succeed only in holding meetings and generating procedural nonsense, and butterflies are symbols of deep and joyful wisdom, readers would doubtless hope to get a butterfly and not a wheel.

Several problems are raised by Yeats's binary offer. One lies in the suggestion that the collection offers two gifts exclusive of each other, dullness to a set of appropriately tedious readers and delight to "a friend." Clearly, few buyers of the book would hope to be fall into the first category, and there is only one other gift on offer. Anyone not admitting to being thickheaded would need to be among Yeats's friends. Nor does this "friend" mean something like "Friends, Romans, countrymen" or "dear reader," an implication of likemindedness that has been part of formal rhetoric at least since Aristotle, and of literary fiction at least since Jane Austen. Readers may think of themselves as sympathetic or skeptical, lovers of poetry, or even the kinds of people who *might* be Yeats's friends if they only knew him, but those other identities are not the ones Yeats told Shakespear were those for whom he "writes & works." It would seem to follow that insofar as wisdom is available only outside those airless spaces, we might not have access to it.

Neither the author nor his publisher would have hoped that sales would be restricted to that select constituency, of course. Nonetheless, this is a binary system, wheels or butterflies. Thus, reading the introductions is a bit uncomfortable: as we turn the pages, we suspect ourselves to be narrow-minded fanatics, voices raised in some rented room in a basement or attic about whatever cause obsesses us—though the primary focus is indeed, as Yeats indicated to Shakespear, "Ireland mainly," a small coterie of Irish readers who form what Yeats calls in the introduction to *Fighting the Waves* "our small public" (*W&B* 64, *VPl* 68). Thus, Yeats refers to "Cellars and Garrets" at third-person distance. The introduction to *The Cat and the Moon*, for example, begins curiously by recommending that the previous play, *The Resurrection*, is inappropriate for them.

> These plays, which substitute speech and music for painted scenery, should suit Cellars and Garrets, though I do not recommend *The Resurrection* to the more pious Communist or Republican cellars; it may not be as orthodox as I think; I recommend *The Cat and the Moon*, for no audience could discover its dark, mythical secrets (*W&B* 121, *VPl* 805–6).

A few pages further, Yeats recalls writing the play. He discloses his goal of secrecy, that "though I might discover what had been and might be again an abstract idea, no abstract idea must be present" in the action of *The Cat and the Moon*. "The spectator should come away thinking the meaning as much his own manufacture as that of the blind man and the lame man had seemed mine" (*W&B* 124, *VPl* 807). The rest of the section then explains the very abstract ideas that would be invisible to this mythical spectator, perhaps a member of "the Gaelic League, or some like body" (*W&B* 123, *VPl* 807).

Here as in the other introductions, the identity of the reader is at issue. The spectator now, years after the play was originally written and produced (in 1926), may be no more able to penetrate the "dark, mythical secrets" of the drama than before, but she certainly has access to those occult spaces, through this introduction and related texts, including *A Vision*. Perhaps she will have read this introduction and thus recognize that the play's "flightiness"—the term that Akiko Manabe parses in her essay in this volume—contributes to an Irish "intellectual nationalism," to use Yeats's phrase in the letter to Shakespear (*CL InteLex* 5414). The author who addresses this reader in the four introductions is urgent but also curiously indirect, preferring metaphor to direct description and backing off from clear assertion to an eclectic array of inter-texts. The persona suggested by this voice is eccentric, even outlandish, but he seems also to make proposals that are, to use a word that Yeats hated, sincere. For example, the first introduction, to *The Words upon the Window-Pane*, puts forward the idea that Ireland should reject the idea of progress:

> I suggest to the Cellars and Garrets that though history is too short to change either the idea of progress or the eternal circuit into scientific fact, the eternal circuit may best suit our preoccupation with the soul's salvation, our individualism, our solitude. Besides we love antiquity, and that other idea— progress—the sole religious myth of modern man, is only two hundred years old (*W&B* 18, *VPl* 963).

The rejection of progress is a theme that had preoccupied Yeats for decades, so the thought is clearly genuine. At the same time, the suggestion that Ireland abandon progress for the idea of eternal return is unlikely, to say the least. Is this projector seriously propounding that the nation exchange Christian teleology for the cyclical Platonic Year, or modern assumptions of development for the eternal oscillation of opposites? The practical absurdity is underscored by the concession that "scientific fact" is unfortunately not available as proof—as if "scientific fact" were useful or relevant—followed by the additional argument that it would suit our character since "we love antiquity."

Although the style of the introductions varies somewhat, even within a single essay, it seems reasonable to treat them as a whole. A single reader may be presumed for the volume *Wheels and Butterflies*, and a single persona or mask is enacted throughout the four essays. That the first essay is haunted by Jonathan Swift is not accidental, though Yeats's proposer is not as harshly Juvenalian as Swift's. The most influential predecessor for Yeats's mode may be Plato and the *eiron* of Socrates in the *Dialogues*, as Stephen Helmling has remarked of *A Vision*.[2] Given the way that the introductions ramble from personal anecdote to political theory to spiritualism to poetry, Menippean satire also comes to mind.[3] At any rate, this speech is double-voiced, unsystematic, and creative. In other words, these wheels may have something of the butterfly in them after all.

Generally speaking, the introductions are strongly rhetorical, even if their style is full of sinuous syntax, qualifying phrases like "perhaps" or "as it were," and seeming divagations. The logic is allusive and anecdotal rather than formal, but the fervor in the tone is unmistakable. The essays express themes that are dear to Yeats in this late period, such as the virtues of eighteenth-century Anglo-Ireland and the spiritual awareness of premodern Irish peasant life, the Platonic Great Year, and life after death. In other words, Yeats's projector may actually share our garret or cellar with us.

There are moments of pure satire, starting with the Preface:

> All these plays have been played at the Abbey Theatre, Dublin. *The Words upon the Window-pane* has been revived several times, *The Cat and the Moon* once, but *Fighting the Waves*, which drew large audiences, not at all, because Mr. George Antheil's most strange, most dramatic music requires a large expensive orchestra. A memory of that orchestra has indeed roused a distinguished Irish lyric poet to begin a dance play which he assures me requires but a tin whistle and a large expensive concertina. *The Resurrection* was played for the first time at the Abbey a few days ago. Like *The Cat and the Moon* it was not intended for the public theatre. I permitted it there after great hesitation. Owing perhaps to a strike which has prevented the publication of the religious as well as of the political newspapers and reviews, all is well.
>
> W. B. Y.
>
> *4th August 1934 (W&B v)*

Besides the farcical detail of the nameless "distinguished Irish lyric poet" who is writing a dance play for tin whistle and "large expensive concertina," the equal-opportunity dig at politics and religion in the last sentence is particularly noteworthy. Later, in the introduction to *The Resurrection*, this theme returns. After recounting episodes in which attempts to rethink both orthodox Marxism and Roman Catholicism, respectively, were shut down by Lenin and Pope Pius X, Yeats comments, "So far I have the sympathy of the Garrets and Cellars, for they are, I am told, without exception Catholic, Communist, or both!" (*W&B* 94, *VPl* 933).

The next sentence brings up "a third myth or philosophy that has made an equal stir in the world," that third myth being the Platonic Year and the eternal waxing and waning of gyres: "there was everywhere a conflict like that of my play between two principles or 'elemental forms of the mind,' each 'living the other's life, dying the other's death'" (*W&B* 95, *VPl* 933–4). With this turn, the introduction to *The Resurrection* leads to a path familiar to all readers of late Yeats: the system of *A Vision*. Does the Platonic Year and the idea of the "re-birth of the soul" actually make "an equal stir in the world" to Marxist politics and Christian religion, and provide an effective counter to their claims? Certainly not recently, at any rate. Yeats proceeds to buttress his points with a number of famous names, citing "empirical evidence like that Lafcadio Hearn found among the Japanese" (*W&B* 96, *VPl* 934) and similar beliefs by Schopenhauer, Hegel, McTaggart, Cardinal Mercier, von Hügel, and of course Plato and Plotinus.

In the midst of this list of august thinkers is an odd interjection: a dash in mid-sentence and then the clause "—I think of that Professor's daughter in Palermo." The eighteenth-century Irish philosopher Francis Hutcheson described this kind of humor, which relies on incongruity: canonical thinkers are put into a list with a medical doctor from Palermo named Camelo Samonà, who wrote an account in 1911 about the reincarnation of his young daughter Allesandrina into one of a set of twins he and his wife Adela conceived soon after Allesandrina's death.[4]

This is a representative sample of Yeats's prose in his late years: the authorial voice is making excessive, even obsessive claims. As problematic as it may be, this tone is deliberate. It is the authorial stance Yeats chose for the pamphlet *On the Boiler*, which takes its name from a man named McCoy, a "mad ship's carpenter" who was given to climbing atop an old rusted boiler in Sligo to "read the Scriptures and denounce his neighbours" (*CW5* 220). The wheelwright in *Wheels and Butterflies* shares a number of characteristics with the persona of "the Great McCoy" or his close kin, the raging old man in *The Death of Cuchulain*, another figure of a "wild old wicked man" from this period. These troublesome works present similar questions of writerly persona and readership to the essays in *Wheels and Butterflies*.

In many of the late plays and poems, tragedy is connected to joy. Near the end of *On the Boiler*, Yeats writes:

> Some Frenchman has said that farce is the struggle against a ridiculous object, comedy against a movable object, tragedy against an immovable; and because the will, or energy, is greatest in tragedy, tragedy is the more noble; but I add that "will or energy is eternal delight," and when its limit is reached it may become a pure, aimless joy, though the man, the shade, still mourns his lost object (*CW5* 247).

I have argued here that the wheels of *Wheels and Butterflies* fall into a mode best described as comedy, or even farce, in opposition to the tragedy of the plays (three of them, at least: *The Cat and the Moon* is an interestingly different case, using comedy and even farce but representing joy). A number of works of prose from Yeats's late period, such as *On the Boiler* and both versions of *A Vision*, also embody this mode. Insofar as Yeats creates a readership for the prose as well as readers and audiences for the plays, it seems we who turn the pages of *Wheels and Butterflies* have a comic fate as well. We may not be his friends, but he and we are caught together in these wheels.

It is worth recalling that Yeats was at this time also engaged in years of work on revising *A Vision*, thinking he was almost finished and being thwarted by that thorny book yet again. He was not only engaged in the system while sitting at his desk: the gyres upon which it is based require that its ideas be lived as well as thought, experienced as well as imagined. The system depends upon polarities in continuous opposition to each other and continuous motion towards each other as well. They move like magnets working from both poles simultaneously, repelled and also attracted to each other, until they reach a point of saturation or vacuum at which they change places. Butterfly drags road metal; wheels pull back brightness from the Zodiac (to steal phrases from the poems "The Fascination of What's Difficult" and "A First Confession"). Again, in the introduction to *The Words upon the Window-Pane*, the first in *Wheels and Butterflies*, Yeats writes that "If the Garrets and the Cellars listen I may throw light upon the matter [of imagination and civic life], and I hope if all the time I seem thinking of something else I shall be forgiven" (*W&B* 6, *VPl* 957). The "something else" is the system, described in the introduction to *The Resurrection* thus: "For years I have been preoccupied with a certain myth that was itself a reply to a myth" (*W&B* 91, *VPl* 932).

So here is a book of contrasts, in the quaternities that fill *A Vision*: four imaginative works and four essays, four dedications to symbolic people, and four emblems (house, mask, sword, and ship). The dates of first performance are prominently displayed on the half title pages for each play, and together they form a sort of inner gyre surrounded by an outer one (1930 and 1929, then a wider spread of dates, 1934 and 1926). Each play mixes high and low speech, poetry and prose, serious and comic modes, and the phenomenal and supernatural worlds. Within the quaternities are the triads explored in the essays that follow this introduction: Swift, Vanessa, and Stella; Cuchulain, Emer, and Eithne Inguba; the Greek, the Hebrew, and the Syrian; the Lame Beggar, the Blind Beggar, and the Saint.[5]

You will guess what I am suggesting: that Yeats created *Wheels and Butterflies* to be an example of the gyres of the visionary system, which feature always-spinning opposites in an endless dance of contrapuntal energy. By this point in his life, Yeats was living and working on a paradigm requiring the energies of both attraction and repulsion, joy and hate, creative and expository writing, intellectual abstraction and biography or personal memory, tragedy and comedy. What this means further is that to appreciate Yeats in the 1930s is to accept this larger picture. Readers should be willing to dive under the wheels as well as enjoy the butterflies of his harsh and beautiful late work. Yeats's definition of tragedy, comedy, and farce from *On the Boiler* can help us to understand the book *Wheels and Butterflies*: "I add that 'will or energy is eternal delight,' and when its limit is reached it may become a pure, aimless joy, though the man, the shade, still mourns his lost object" (*CW5* 247).

NOTES

1   *Wheels and Butterflies* (London: Macmillan, 1934; New York: Macmillan, 1935), henceforward abbreviated *W&B*. The plays and introductions are also included in *VPl*; page numbers will refer to *VPl* as well as the US edition of *W&B*.

2   On *A Vision* as comedy or satire, see Steven Helmling, *The Esoteric Comedies of Carlyle, Newman, and Yeats* (Cambridge: Cambridge University Press, 1988); Eugene Korkowski, "Yeats's *Vision* as Philosophic *Satura*," *Eire-Ireland* 12, no. 3 (Fomhar/Autumn 1977): 62–70; Hazard Adams, *The Book of Yeats's Vision: Romantic Modernism and Antithetical Tradition* (Ann Arbor: University of Michigan Press, 1995); and Elizabeth Muller, "The Mask of Derision in Yeats's Prologue to *A Vision* (1937), in *YA19*, eds. Margaret Mills Harper and Warwick Gould (Cambridge: Open Book Publishers, 2013): 121–46.

3   Northrop Frye famously used this term in his categorization of literary genres, although he did not associate it with Yeats. Frye considered *A Vision* a serious epic, if one for an ironic age. See *Anatomy of Criticism: Four Essays* (1957; repr., Princeton, NJ: Princeton University Press, 2000). See also Frye, "Yeats and the Language of Symbolism," in *Fables of Identity: Studies in Poetic Mythology* (New York: Harcourt Brace and World, 1963), 218–37.

4   I do not know where Yeats encountered this narrative, but it would have appealed to him in part because of a detail involving a state between lives. According to Karen Wehrstein, writing for the *Psi Encyclopaedia*:

> Carmelo Samonà, a physician in Palermo, Italy, and his wife Adele lost their daughter Alessandrina to meningitis on March 10, 1910, when she was five. Three days later, Adele had the first of two dreams in which Alessandrina reassured her that she was not gone and would return.

The couple heard from Alessandrina as well as "Carmelo's sister Giannina, who had died many years before," with a promise of Alessandrina's return. In April, Adele discovered that she was pregnant, and with twins, as the spirits had foretold. The new daughter exhibited the same "quietness, little interest in toys, phobias of barbers, a dislike of cheese, a fascination with playing with cloth and shoes, a tendency to refer to herself in the third person, and left-handedness" as her predecessor. The other daughter, named Maria Pace, had not been part of the family in a past life, but the two spirits were understood to have "agreed in the intermission" between lives to return together as twins. See Wehrstein, "People Who Knew Each Other in Past Lives," *Psi Encyclopedia* (London: The Society for Psychical Research, 2017), retrieved May 14, 2020, https://psi-encyclopedia.spr.ac.uk/articles/people-who-knew-each-other-past-lives

5   It may be worth noting that the twenty-eight lunar phases that are one of the principle symbols of *A Vision* may be described as triads within quaternities. See, for example, Table 12.1 in Neil Mann, *A Reader's Guide to Yeats's* A Vision (Clemson, SC: Clemson University Press, 2019), 216–18.

CORNERED: INTIMATE RELATIONS IN *THE WORDS UPON THE WINDOW-PANE*

Charles I. Armstrong

When *Wheels and Butterflies* was published by Macmillan in 1934, both the cover and the title page featured an image of three faces clustered together in a circular formation. This image was based on theatrical masks made by the Dutch artist Hildo van Krop for *The Only Jealousy of Emer* and subsequently used in a Dublin production of *Fighting the Waves* (a dance play based on *The Only Jealousy of Emer*). The masks belong to the characters of the Woman of the Sidhe, Emer, and Cuchulain, and their juxtaposition on the cover reflects the complex love triangle in *Fighting the Waves*.[1] Set in intimate proximity, the three partially overlapping faces appear anguished and awkwardly, even forcibly intertwined. Although originally written and staged in 1930, *The Words upon the Window-Pane* was—like *Fighting the Waves*—one of the four plays included in the *Wheels and Butterflies* volume. The cover image also speaks to *The Words upon the Window-Pane*, which circles around the historical circumstances of Jonathan Swift's amatory relationships to Vanessa and Stella at the beginning of the eighteenth century.

Love is not simply a particular theme or motif in literature. It transcends the status of mere content in a literary text. Towards the end of his career, Harold Bloom reformulated his famous thesis concerning the anxiety of influence. Influence, he claimed in *The Anatomy of Influence: Literature as a Way of Life*, was a matter of *"literary love."*[2] Whereas Bloom in his early writings had theorized the relationship between a strong writer and his exemplary forerunners as an Oedipal battle, at this late stage he was willing to admit that literary influence could be put in more positive terms. Whether or not Bloom's later writings can be said to fundamentally adjust his earlier theory, the idea of literary love is of some use in making sense of *The Words upon the Window-Pane*; but rather than looking exclusively at narrowly defined love relationships in this essay, I reflect on a wider range of relationships that can be defined as relations of intimacy. By this I mean relationships of love or proximity that undermine autonomy and that commit subjectivity—both spatially and interpersonally—beyond itself. This in turn relates to the idea of a relational, vulnerable self as formulated by Judith Butler.[3] Among several relevant post-structuralist rearticulations of subjectivity, also worthy of mention is Jean-Luc Nancy's notion of exposed being, which is formulated in regards to both signification and love. "'To be exposed,'" Nancy writes, "means to be 'posed' in exteriority, according to an exteriority, having to do with an outside *in the very intimacy* of an inside."[4] For Nancy, the fundamentally exposed nature of subjectivity is intrinsically also a relation of representation—thus not merely a relation of "juxtaposition, but exposition."[5]   Nancy renounces, however, the idea of creating a master narrative or general theory of love relations or community, and this essay will not attempt to subsume Yeats's play under any overarching concept or theoretical regime.

This article hypothesizes that the tortured love relationships between Swift, Stella, and Vanessa are not without relevance to Yeats's appropriation of Swift. In addition, I place these examples of erotic and literary intimacy alongside the play's dramatization of a séance. Love, literature, and mediumship, I claim, enter into interesting connections—indeed, in relations of intimacy—in the play. Interpersonal relations and representational strategies are interlinked, rather than a set of loosely collected devices. Both the interpersonal relations and the representational processes in question frequently involve spatial relations of proximity, and one of this essay's key arguments focuses on how *The Words upon the Window-Pane* self-consciously addresses notions of place and space. More abstractly, this kind of spatial proximity amounting to a form of overlapping also shows itself on the textual plane, as Yeats's play enters into close but far from unequivocal relations with its introduction in *Wheels and Butterflies* and the posthumously published "Pages from a Diary in 1930," as well as other texts by Yeats and parts of Swift's *oeuvre*. In all of these instances, my interpretation demonstrates relations of a kind of cornered intimacy, even if I do not pretend to have cornered (i.e., hunted down and brought under control) any univocal, underlying meaning subsuming the singular vitality of the play and its relations.

Yeats wrote *The Words upon the Window-Pane* quickly, starting to plan the play in August 1930 and finishing it in early October that same year. This creative burst followed a long period of illness, with Yeats suffering from brucellosis ("Malta fever") for several months, attended by his wife George and hired nurses, in Rapallo and nearby Portofina Vetta. In December 1929, the situation was sufficiently serious for Yeats to dictate a will. During his confinement, both Yeats and George led extremely enclosed and limited lives. In a letter to Lennox Robinson, George lamented that except for "balconies I haven't been out I really forget for how long [...]. What's happened to the world?"[6] She also complained about the proximity and the personality of the nurses, whose presence was no doubt experienced as both a support for, and an encroachment upon, the married couple's domestic togetherness.

During his recovery in the spring, Yeats wrote to L. A. G. Strong:

> I am almost well again—indeed there is nothing wrong now except that I tire very soon. After five months of illness I have begun to work again though but

a little and not every day. I have had much illness these last two years, but there seems no reason why I should not now be as well as ever (April 15, 1930, CL *InteLex* 5344).

Yeats put up a bluff façade in his letters, but it is obvious that this period of confinement had been extremely difficult. To Lennox Robinson he wryly described himself as having emerged from "a kind of happy prison" (February 28, 1930, CL *InteLex* 5335), and in a letter to George Russell (AE) he underscored the physical toll of prolonged isolation:

I have been ill for five months, and blink at the world as if fresh from the cloister. My wife tells me that the little wrinnckles [sic] are gone out of my face. All days or nights of discomfort or delirium have been blotted from my memory and I recall nothing but peace (April 13, 1930, CL *InteLex* 5342).

Already, at this point, Yeats was looking back at his ill self as something of a stranger, and he was not particularly anxious to dwell on an experience in which (to quote Virginia Woolf's "On Being Ill") "the world has changed its shape; the tools of business grown remote."[7] But still the memory of a different kind of existence, akin to that of a "prison" or a "cloister" where nothing can be done, impinged upon his consciousness, and the play he would go on to write after his recovery would pay implicit testimony to that memory.

When *The Words upon the Window-Pane* was first staged by the Abbey in November 1930, it became something of a surprise success. Unusually for Yeats, it did well at the box office. While this was notable enough, it must have come as surprise, perhaps especially to Yeats himself, that a play based on his interests in the esoteric had found such a wide and seemingly receptive audience. The play deploys mediumship and the séance in a more direct fashion than any other of Yeats's dramatic writings. In doing so, it articulates a desire for intimacy that underpins mediumship. Séances often involve the wish of bereaved individuals to get in touch with their lost loved ones. In *The Words upon the Window-Pane*, Mrs. Mallet is in this position: she wants to speak to her deceased husband, as she declares she will remain "utterly lost" if she "cannot question him" (*CW2* 469).

Mediumship, as portrayed in Yeats's play, involves an attempt to make the dead speak. This parallels Yeats's own relationship to Swift. Like the other plays published in *Wheels and Butterflies*, *The Words upon the Window-Pane* was coupled with a prose introduction providing a contextualization of the text. The introduction presents Swift as a key figure who "created the political nationality of Ireland" in the *Drapier's Letters* (*CW2* 710), while also suggesting that he was a witness to the breaking apart of pre-modern harmony. I will return to the prose introduction later, but for now I want to dwell on the following words: "Swift haunts me, he is always just round the next corner" (*CW2* 708). Yeats immediately links this compulsion not only to personal connections (i.e., an ancestor who was in the ambit of Swift's social circles) but also to his own experiences, wandering around St. Patrick's Cathedral and other parts of Dublin, amidst an urban landscape that seemed to bear the traces of Swift and his contemporaries. In this setting, he wrote, the past spoke to him as something that was "near and yet hidden" (*CW2* 708). In *W. B. Yeats and Georgian Ireland*, Donald Torchiana claims that Yeats's sense of being haunted indicates the strength of Yeats's admiration for Swift—the fact that, in Torchiana's words, "Swift had always attracted him."[8] This is perhaps overstating things, as Yeats early on in his career had little time for Swift and other eighteenth-century figures, in contrast with his strong admiration for the Romantics. As he writes earlier in the same text: "I turned from Goldsmith and from Burke because they had come to seem a part of the English system, from Swift because I acknowledged, being a romantic, no verse between Cowley and Smart's *Song to David*, no prose between Sir Thomas Browne and the *Conversations* of Landor" (*CW2* 707). His feelings would change by 1930, yet his admission, "Swift haunts me," should not be construed simply as an expression of newfound attraction or admiration. Rather, I suggest, in setting this quotation alongside the play, that Yeats's relationship with Swift was akin to that of a medium with a spirit. I further propose that the reference to Swift's being "just round the next corner" is significant and connects with other references to inaccessibility—to things that are near and yet unreachable—in the play.

The Words upon the Window-Pane portrays a contemporary séance in which the medium Mrs. Henderson unwittingly channels Swift and the two key women of his adult life, Esther Johnson (dubbed "Stella" by Swift himself) and Esther Vanhomrigh (also called "Vanessa"). Their medium, Mrs. Henderson, and her mediumistic control, Lulu, experience these figures as frustrators who get in the way of the real business of the séance for the rather motley crowd attending.[9] The odd one out at the séance is the young Cambridge student John Corbet, who happens to be writing a Ph.D. on Swift and his relationship with Stella. When Dr. Trench hands Corbet a scrap of paper showing the lines of verse etched on the window-pane, which are traditionally ascribed to Stella, the young scholar has no difficulty recalling the poem and the circumstances of its composition. This prompts Dr. Trench to remark: "I have shown that writing to several persons, and you are the first who has recognized the lines" (*CW2* 468). Corbet also recognizes the poem when Swift, channeled by Mrs. Henderson, quotes it at greater length in his speech to Stella later on in the séance (see *CW2* 476). Based on his knowledge of Swift's life story, he sees in the details of the unfolding drama an accurate reconstruction of past events but dismisses the séance itself as an elaborate fabrication on the part of Mrs. Henderson. This is a missed opportunity, as the possibility for witness and recognition is introduced but goes unfulfilled. Indeed, Corbet is reminiscent of the Greek in Yeats's play *The Resurrection*, also included in *Wheels and Butterflies*. There, the Greek is yet another figure whose rationalism makes it impossible to place credence in the supernatural events that take place in his presence—although, as some scholars have pointed out, *The Words upon the Window-Pane* can be read as casting some doubt upon the actual veracity of its apparitions.[10]

If there is a breakdown in communication between the spirit of Swift and the participants in the séance, there are also complications in Swift's intimate relations. By way of Mrs. Henderson and Lulu, he is revealed to be in the middle of a tortured love triangle. In the first dramatized sequence, he confronts Vanessa, scolding her for having questioned Stella about an alleged secret marriage between her and Swift. For Swift, Vanessa should be above such things, yet rather than acting with the dignity of a Cato or Brutus, she has been behaving "like some common slut with her ear against the keyhole" (*CW2* 474). In other words, a crisis in Swift's personal affairs has been unleashed through a transgression of the spatial confines of domesticity.

At this point in the play, the audience has become familiarized with the enclosed space of the stage. While the way in which the stage is used might remind one of the "conventional stage realism" of Ibsen, Shaw, and other realists,[11] the dynamics of Yeats's play go beyond such a framework. The exposition of the play depicts in some detail the arrival of all the participants at the séance, with knockings on the door and scenes of welcoming, as they enter the building via an entrance hall. At the end they all depart, leaving only Mrs. Henderson, who, unknown even to herself, is still under the spell of Swift. The seemingly unremarkable locality has deeper resonances. *The Words upon the Window-Pane* is dedicated "In Memory of / Lady Gregory / In Whose House It Was Written" (CW2 465). Although she was still alive when the play was first staged, by the time it was published in *Wheels and Butterflies*, Lady Gregory was dead. In "Pages from a Diary in 1930," written at the same time as the play, Yeats foresees the ignominious future of his friend's Big House: "Coole as a Gregory house is near its end, it will be before long an office and residence for foresters, a little cheap furniture in the great room, a few religious oleographs its only pictures" (*Ex* 319). One might compare this anticipated non-place with the setting of the play. Dr. Trench observes that the building used for the séance was once inhabited by Stella and "was a country-house in those days, surrounded by trees and gardens" (*CW2* 467). The building still has "large stables at the back" (*CW2* 467), but it has been swallowed up by the urban sprawl of the city and is now a mere lodging house. Implicitly, there is a tacit parallel between the fall of Georgian Dublin and the impending demise of twentieth-century Ascendancy culture.

The premises are effectively a haunted house (as is made even clearer in drafts of the play, where J. Sheridan Le Fanu is mentioned), and desire is dramatized as being baulked by spatial confines. Swift is first introduced by Lulu as "[t]hat bad man, that bad old man in the corner" (*CW2* 473). His exposed position "in the corner" is a physical manifestation of his dislocation. Like Oedipus, who in *Oedipus at Colonus* has been "driven out to wander through my whole life as a beggar and an outcast" (*CW2* 412), Swift is a figure at the extreme margins of community. Both Oedipus and Swift have transgressed sexual mores and are paying a steep price. "Never to have lived is best," the chorus of *Oedipus at Colonus* says (*CW2* 432), while Yeats's Swift cries out: "Perish the day on which I was born!" (*CW2* 479). Whereas Oedipus is hovering outside the borders of the *polis*, though, the Dean of St. Patrick's Cathedral is banished from the realm of the living. When the participants in the séance join together in singing John Keble's words in a hymn, asking that "some poor wandering child of Thine / […] no more [must] lie down in sin" (*CW2* 475), they are praying for his absolution. But there is no transcendence for Swift analogous to that which "fixes our amazed attention" on Oedipus "when his death approaches" at the end of the *Oedipus at Colonus* (*Ex* 299), no end to his wanderings. He is cornered and simply cannot find a way out.

In the following dramatization of the relationship between Vanessa and Swift, the confines hemming both in are evident in her frustrated desire to attain complete intimacy. "I thought it would be enough to look at you," she tells Swift, "to speak to you, to hear you speak. I followed you to Ireland five years ago and I can bear it no longer. It is not enough to look, to speak, to hear" (*CW2* 474). In the earliest existing draft of the play, in a notebook Yeats kept in Rapallo, Vanessa's language is even more repetitive and desperate: "It is not enough to see you," she says, "It is not enough to see enough, not enough to see & speak to you, not enough to see & speak, & touch your hands when we meet or part."[12] She grasps his hand and places it on her breast, in a moment of tense erotic proximity, but Swift resists. He is shown to be torn between his strong passion and a concern about the possible offspring of their relationship. He is also judgmental, flaunting an intellectual superiority that has led A. S. Knowland to characterize him as "an intellectual corner-boy."[13] Significantly, this passage ends with Swift being unable to escape due to Dr. Trench having earlier locked the door: "Who locked the door?" he asks, "who locked me in with my enemy?" (*CW2* 475). The locked room becomes an image of his repeated, unredeemed trauma, which is only heightened by the way in which he is exposed to an ignorant group attending a séance. They too are cornered, forced to submit to a confusing presence that interrupts their session.

When Stella's relationship to Swift unfolds in the subsequent part of the play, she is not portrayed as an erotically charged figure and thus presents a contrast to Vanessa. Swift's two loves embody the penury and excess of passion, respectively, rather than any idealized view of consummated love. Earlier in the play we have come across a couplet from Stella's poem "To Dr. Swift on his Birthday, November 30, 1721"—these are the words upon the window-pane. Singled out in the title of Yeats's play, the word "window-pane" brings associations of isolation and the necessity of having to make do with representations: rather than having direct access to reality, one has to make do with a distanced view from afar. The emotive disturbance caused by this sense of constriction is also hinted at in the homonym of "pain." Unlike the inscription discovered by Lockwood at the beginning of Emily Brontë's *Wuthering Heights*, the actual words inscribed in Yeats's play do not herald the unveiling of a passionate, stormy relationship. Instead, the relationship between Stella and Swift is portrayed as being affectionate but distant.

Swift mainly engages with Stella through textual exegesis, as her own voice is not channeled. Stella's poem presents a version of the nineteenth-century notion of the beautiful soul, where inner virtue is reflected by outer beauty.[14] Although Swift tries to put a positive gloss on their relationship, his denial of bodily intimacy reduces her to a wan, sexless shadow: Stella is an isolated, stunted figure. As such she is a connecting link with Lady Gregory's granddaughter, Anne Gregory, in Yeats's poem "For Anne Gregory." This poem was written alongside *The Words upon the Window-Pane* in Yeats's Rapallo notebook and has a related theme of imperfect human love. Where no suitor, but only God, can offer transcendent love, mortals are exposed to a state of lack. In the words of Swift's character in Yeats's play: "You have no children, you have no lover, you have no husband" (*CW2* 476).

In "Pages from a Diary in 1930," Yeats suggests that Swift "almost certainly hated sex" (*Ex* 334). This abnegation of physical relations is certainly important in the play: Swift cannot deny his physical urges yet nevertheless struggles to abstain from pursuing them. For Terence Brown, "the biographical force of the work is to be found in its conviction that the tragedy of Swift, expiring a driveller and a show, was a sexual tragedy. To deny the body, as Yeats had done for so many years in his young manhood, was to tempt a Swiftian fate, as he now understood."[15] Although Brown here draws an interesting parallel with the young Yeats's struggle to remain chaste, it is hard to believe that personal memories dating thirty or forty years back in time might provide a key clue to decipher what is a complex, many-cornered play. The play's focus on a love triangle might instead lead one to Yeats's persistent questioning of marriage and domestic bliss in favor of more bohemian relations, insisting upon an excess that challenges conventional ideas of monogamy.[16] Although most overtly a feature of his writings prior to his marriage to Georgie Hyde Lees in 1917, this dimension more implicitly enters Yeats's oeuvre via his later balancing of that marriage with extramarital affairs and flirtations. The position of Swift in the play, caught between the youthful advances of Vanessa and the long-suffering loyalty of Stella, can be compared to that of Cuchulain in *Fighting the Waves*. The previously mentioned use of masks representing Cuchulain, Emer, and Eithne Inguba on the cover of *Wheels and Butterflies* might be motivated by the similar love relationships of these two central plays of that volume.[17] In addition to the dynamics of their erotic relationships, Cuchulain and Swift are figures who languish in a kind of ghostly twilight zone between life and death. Both are also characters whose identity is usurped by stand-ins: Cuchulain's by Bricriu who has taken his "likeness" (*CW2* 459) and Swift's by the mediating presences of Mrs. Henderson and Lulu.

Swift's situation is of course shared, in this respect, with his two loves. The relay of voices in *The Words upon the Window-Pane* underscores Stella's isolation. Her voice is subject to multiple mediation: it comes to us via the medium of Mrs. Henderson, who channels it via Lulu, who again mediates Swift, who for his part passes on not Stella's own words but rather those of her poem. The words upon the window-pane are thus a figure of erasure in the play, poetry being a particularly a weak form of representation in this work. This is not the only meta-literary reference in Yeats's play. The way in which Swift, Stella, and Vanessa have reappeared in Mrs. Henderson's séances leads Mrs. Mallet, early on, to say that it is "just as if they were characters in some kind of play" (*CW2* 469). In his introduction to *The Words upon the Window-Pane*, Mrs. Henderson's role persuades Yeats to insist that "mediumship is dramatization" (CW2 719). This claim would in turn cause a rather worried correspondence between him and George, who interpreted it as being more suggestive of mere fabrication than a true manifestation of spirits.[18] Certainly, the play raises rather open-ended questions about the force and veracity of Swift's presence. In his introduction to the play, Yeats reads him as representative of a civilization that is already being threatened by degeneration. In the words of Corbet in the first draft of the play, "Swift was not only the greatest literary figure of the age but as it were its symbol."[19] The symbol is to accomplish an act of *symballein* (to use the ancient Greek verb), the bringing together or touching of the individual figure and its more general, historical significance. With regard to *The Words upon the Window-Pane*, Corbet is very much the mediating figure that is entrusted with bringing together these two dimensions, linking the concrete action of the play with the historical exegesis provided in Yeats's prose introduction in *Wheels and Butterflies*. Yeats cannot but endorse Swift's rejection of Vanessa, since it confirms his higher mission as a representative figure of the eighteenth-century Protestant Ascendancy. This rejection makes Yeats's relationship to Swift possible: Vanessa's loss is Yeats's gain. The strong investment he places in that relationship is hinted at in the way Yeats refers to the play in his letters to

George. On September 14, 1930, he calls it simply "the Swift play" (*CL InteLex* 5382). By October 4 of the same year, he refers to it as "Swift or as I call it 'Words Upon the Window Pane'" (*CL InteLex* 5391). In subsequent letters he would periodically mention "Window Pane," but on October 22, 1931 he refers to it, in his commentary on the play (first published in a shorter form in the *Dublin Magazine*), as "my Swift" (*CL InteLex* 5526).

Yeats's strong personal investment is also evident in how he negotiates the temporal divide that separates him from Swift. Matthew de Forrest has written eloquently about how *The Words upon the Window-Pane* involves a "specific kind of time travel" that relates to *A Vision* and the opposition between eternity and historical time.[20] In his dealings with Swift, however, Yeats also negotiates a traditional hermeneutical dichotomy, key to Victorian predecessors such as Tennyson and Hardy, between the past and present. In "Pages from a Diary in 1930," Yeats reflects upon how "thoughts become more vivid when I find they were thought out in historical circumstances which affect those in which I live, or, which is perhaps the same thing, were thought first by men my ancestors may have known" (*Ex* 293). In the same entry, he goes on to note how a particularity of Swift's style makes it possible for his voice to carry across the chasm of history: "I can hear Swift's voice in his letters speaking the sentences at whatever pace makes their sound and idiom expressive. He speaks and we listen at leisure. [...] Swift wrote for men sitting at table or fireside—from that come his animation and his naturalness" (*Ex* 293–94). Swift excels in striking a vivid pose, one might say, if one also allows for the word's etymological root of positioning or commanding a place.

Yeats's belief in Swift's ability to become present for contemporaries can be compared to how the character of Abraham Johnson, in *The Words upon the Window-Pane*, wishes to draw upon the spirit of the American evangelist Dwight L. Moody. Johnson wants "to ask him to stand invisible beside me when I speak or sing, and lay his hands upon my head and give me such a portion of his power that my work may be blessed" (*CW2* 469). Apart from the reference to touching, which anticipates the frustrated bodily contact between Vanessa and Swift later in the play, it is worth pausing at the use of the word "portion" here. In the Harvard manuscript version of the text, the word was written in a near-illegible hand, forcing the typist to leave an empty space. This in turn meant that Yeats had to re-insert the word in the typescript by hand. "Portion" is not a word much used in Yeats's writings, but it shows up in the poem "Broken Dreams," where Yeats writes of the great "portion" Heaven has in the peace Maud Gonne makes "By merely walking in a room" (*CW1* 153). In both these cases, then, "portion" conveys a form of embodied representation— even while its privative nature (a portion, instead of the whole) indicates that the representative vehicle is missing or incomplete. The hymn sung at the beginning of the séance relates to this issue. The participants sing the following lines from the opening of John Keble's hymn 564: "Sun of my soul, Thou Saviour dear, / It is not night if Thou be near: / O may no earth-born cloud arise / To hide Thee from Thy servant's eyes" (*CW2* 479). God's presence is desired in the same way as that of other spiritual beings in the play.

In Yeats's relationship to Swift, privation is caused by temporal distance. Yeats desires a form of immediate contact with Swift, which will close the gap between past and present. He further explores how to facilitate such contact in an extraordinary passage in the introduction to the play:

> In judging any moment of past time we should leave out what has since happened; we should not call the Swift of the *Drapier Letters* nearer truth because of their influence upon history than the Swift who attacked in *Gulliver* the inventors and logicians; we should see certain men and women as if at the edge of a cliff, time broken away from their feet (*CW2* 716).

There is a sense in which this passage is facilitating the atemporal presence with which Yeats often opposed historicism. At the same time, his act of isolating Swift "as if at the edge of a cliff" strategically leaves Yeats face to face with his eighteenth-century inspiration. The passage is reminiscent of a key episode in Thomas Hardy's *A Pair of Blue Eyes*, where Henry Knight's hanging on a cliff leads to an epiphany where "Not a blade, not an insect, which spoke of the present, was between him and the past."[21] It also anticipates a famous passage in Walter Benjamin's 1940 "Theses on the Philosophy of History," where the causal connections and unified narratives of positivist history are said to be countered by an alternative approach whereby Benjamin grasps "the constellation which his own era has formed with a definite earlier one."[22]

The desire to create a "constellation" with Swift and his historical moment entails that Yeats wishes to leap-frog everything that historically can come between them. What the German hermeneutical tradition calls the *Wirkungsgeschichte*, the reception history of the preceding author's life and works, is to be simply bracketed out. Certainly, Swift's relations with Stella and Vanessa have been subject to much later attention. Summing up part of this tradition, Louise Barnett sardonically remarks: "Down through history male critics have gallantly lauded Stella and condemned the importuning Vanessa as a usurper."[23] Thanks to the scholarship of Mary Fitzgerald, we know that Yeats here is more specifically preceded by a significant body of theatrical work in the first decades of the nineteenth century. In an article reprinted, in revised form, as the preface to the Cornell manuscripts edition of *The Words upon the Window-Pane*, Fitzgerald has shown that Yeats's work with the play was facilitated by the pre-existence of earlier plays exploring Swift's personal life.[24]

Fitzgerald mentions Sidney Paternoster's 1913 Abbey play *The Dean of St. Patrick's* but argues for a more significant source: *Swift and Stella: A Play in One Act*, by Charles Edward Lawrence (an acquaintance of both Lady Gregory and Yeats), published in the *Cornhill Magazine* in 1926. In addition to the two texts broached by Fitzgerald, one can also add Florence Bell's 1903 *The Dean of St. Patrick's*. In Bell's play, as in Paternoster's and Lawrence's, much is made of Swift's complicated *ménage à trois*. At one point, one of her characters exclaims: "What! must a man needs have two women at his beck and call to make his life comfortable and put up with his humours, and never a wife with it all to make him hear reason?"[25] This might be compared to John Corbet's observation, made early in *The Words upon the Window-Pane*: "How strange that a celibate scholar, well on in life, should keep the love of two such women!" (*CW2* 468). As all three of the preceding plays circle around the love triangle between Swift, Stella, and Vanessa, this suggests that the choice of the central, intimate relations at the heart of Yeats's play was hardly an innovation in his time. Just as Yeats in his introduction to *The Words upon the Window-Pane* struggles to assert himself and distinguish his own views from those of Corbet and the other characters—"If I had not denied myself, if I had allowed some character to speak my thoughts," he asks at one point, "what would he have said?" (*CW2* 719)—the play embodies Yeats's struggle to articulate a distinct contribution in the midst of a veritable industry of Swift plays. All the more reason for Yeats to call his version "My Swift." His use of this possessive pronoun can however be interpreted as ambiguous. While it indicates that Yeats's appropriation of Swift is his own, singular property, it also implicitly concedes that there are other Swifts that are not Yeats's.

I think this ambivalence corresponds to an undercurrent in Yeats's inclusion of a translation of Swift's epitaph among the poems in *The Winding Stair*. While the epitaph might be read as clearly distinguishing between passersby who are addressed as "World-besotted travelers" and more savvy inheritors such as Yeats, the admonitory "Imitate him if you dare" nevertheless expresses unease (*CW1* 250). For although Swift is portrayed heroically in texts such as "The Tower" and the introduction to *The Words upon the Window-Pane*, the play itself indicates he is not a figure one could emulate or embrace without reserve. Michael McAteer has even gone as far as to claim that the play shows Swift "living out the collapse of his mind as a perpetual curse."[26] To imitate such a man is to flirt with disaster.

What firmly separates Yeats's play from those of Bell, Paternoster, and Lawrence is the way in which the love triangle at its heart is framed by a contemporary séance. If Yeats presents *his* Swift, it is specifically a Swift who struggles to be heard. This structure of blockage and indirection relates, in fact, to a key feature of Swift's career as a writer. As Leo Damrosch writes:

much of Swift's writing was issued under assumed names: Isaac Bickerstaff, M. B., Drapier, Lemuel Gulliver. As with his gift for mimicry, he relished the game of becoming someone very different from himself as he appropriated a voice—people from the lower classes, politicians he despised, household servants, patrician ladies.[27]

Swift's career is full of examples of his speaking through other voices, and as such Yeats's decision to channel him, via Mrs. Henderson and Lulu, paradoxically represents a loyal form of mediation.

An in-depth account of Yeats's deployment of Swiftian sources will not be given here, but there are other aspects of Swift's writings that would seem to suggest that Yeats's séance is no arbitrary imposition upon his eighteenth-century predecessor's example. Although the *Wheels and Butterflies* introduction is mainly devoted to Swift's politics, the vein of pessimistic classicism that runs through his writings may also have played a role in determining how Yeats chose to represent his legacy for a twentieth-century audience. In "On the Death of Dr. Swift," Swift anticipated the lack of any posthumous life for his own work:

One year is past; a different scene;
No further mention of the Dean;
Who now, alas, no more is missed
Than if he never did exist.
Where's now the fav'rite of Apollo?
Departed; and his works must follow:
Must undergo the common fate.
His kind of wit is out of date.[28]

The threat of posthumous neglect appears often in Swift's writings. In the words of "Cadenus and Vanessa," he fears a situation where such "great examples" as his own "are in vain / Where ignorance begets disdain."[29] The way in which even Corbet cannot recognize Swift's presence in *The Words upon the Window-Pane* represents an ironic version of precisely this scenario.

Fighting against neglect, Swift sought to impose his presence upon the reader. While he mercilessly parodied mysticism alongside other forms of unconventional Christianity in *A Tale of the Tub*, Swift also explored how writing could in some ways be said to compensate or obviate the author's lack of immediate presence in his work. In "Cadenus and Vanessa," pedagogy is shown to be heightened when "[t]he book, the author, and the friend" can be said to be one and the same.[30] Ideally, the author communicates through his books in a way that is as immediate as face-to-face contact with a friend. That authorial presence might, in some cases, even survive death. In *The Battle of the*

Books, such survival is part of the lively personification of classic books. There, the way in which authors communicate posthumously in their works is said to be in the form of "a restless spirit" that "haunts over every book."[31] When Yeats states that "Swift haunts me," he is effectively confirming his predecessor's poetics of posthumous survival.

Even during his own lifetime, Swift was not averse to haunting others through his writings. In *The Words upon the Window-Pane*, Dr. Trench mentions that Swift "chaffed" Stella in "the *Journal to Stella* because of certain small sums of money she lost at cards probably in this room" (CW2 467). In some of the more playful passages in his letters from London to Stella and Rebecca Dingley between 1710 and 1713, which were later published as *Journal to Stella*, Swift imagines himself eavesdropping or even haunting Stella during her card games back in Dublin. On March 20, 1711, he teasingly admonishes her:

> [...] so go to your dean's, and roast his oranges, and lose your money, do so, you saucy sluts. Ppt, you lost three shillings and four pence t'other night at Stoite's, yes, you did, and pdfr stood in a corner, and saw you all the while, and then stole away. I dream very often I am in Ireland, and that I have left my cloaths and things behind me, and have not taken leave of any body; and that the ministry expect me to-morrow, and such nonsense.[32]

In passages such as this, Swift uses information he has received from acquaintances of Stella (affectionately referred to as "Ppt", i.e., "Poppet," here) and Dingley to reconstruct their movements and activities in his absence. While he conjures their visits to figures such as John Stearne (then the dean of St. Patrick's) and Dublin alderman John Stoyte, he also imagines himself (frequently identified as "pdfr") as hovering in the vicinity. As an invisible figure standing "in a corner" in this passage, Swift is projecting himself as a ghostlike persona haunting the location where Stella engages in her games of cards. The passage thus prefigures, and may have influenced, Yeats's own imagining of Swift as a "bad old man in the corner" of Stella's former home in *The Words upon the Window-Pane* (CW2 473).

The image of the cornered Dean has been something of a leitmotif in this essay, in which I have explored the relationship between literature, mediumship, and love both within *The Words upon the Window-Pane* and in the play's outer, paratextual ambit. My aim has not been to imply that there exists one master narrative of relationships but rather to show how this fascinating play strongly suggests and demonstrates the analogous ways that various forms of intimacy—from the sexual and social to the literary and spiritual—are experienced. The intense, claustrophobic spatiality of the play is informed by the memory of Yeats's confinement during a long illness in the months preceding its composition, while the focus on Swift speaks to Yeats's own experience of literary influence, a wish to channel a "portion" of his great eighteenth-century Ascendancy precursor, and a form of emotionally charged desire. In Swift's hauntingly intimate relation to Yeats, a double bind of sorts inheres, whereby closeness to Swift is both desired and resisted by the author of *The Words upon the Window-Pane*. Such an ambivalent relation is at the heart of Bloom's notion of the anxiety of influence,[33] and is also, I would suggest, at play in Yeats's late fascination with the Dean. While one might be tempted to see Yeats's use of the framing séance as a betrayal or ironic displacement of Swift's personal love predicament, being stuck between Stella and Vanessa, the concluding part of this essay has told another story. As a writer of indirection, obsessed with both the difficulties and possibilities of representation, Swift's example also informs those parts of the play that might, at first glance, appear most distant from him. Although Yeats's Swift is an unsettlingly vulnerable and exposed character, he is also a remarkably compelling figure, whose vitality draws upon the example of his real-life model.

NOTES

1   For reproductions of the images and an account of how Yeats and his publishers arrived at the final design, see Warwick Gould, "*Wheels and Butterflies*: Title, Structure, Cover Design," in *YA19*, eds. Margaret Mills Harper and Warwick Gould, (Cambridge: Open Book Publishers, 2013), 369–78.

2   Harold Bloom, *The Anatomy of Influence: Literature as a Way of Life* (New Haven, CT and London: Yale University Press, 2011), 8. Italics in the original.

3   See particularly Judith Butler, "Violence, Mourning, Politics," in *Precarious Life: The Powers of Mourning and Violence* (London: Verso, 2004), 19–49.

4   Jean-Luc Nancy, *The Inoperative Community*, ed. Peter Connor, trans. Peter Connor, Lisa Garbus, Michael Holland, and Simona Sawhney (Minneapolis: University of Minnesota Press, 1991), xxxvii. Italics in the original. The spatial dynamics explored in my reading of *The Words upon the Window-Pane* are also related to the issue of framing in Yeats, explored in Charles I. Armstrong, *Reframing Yeats: Genre, Allusion and History* (London: Bloomsbury, 2013).

5   Nancy, *The Inoperative Community*, 29.

6   George Yeats to Lennox Robinson, January 9, 1930, cited in Ann Saddlemyer, *Becoming George: The Life of Mrs. W. B. Yeats* (Oxford: Oxford University Press, 2002), 424.

7   Virginia Woolf, *The Crowded Dance of Modern Life. Selected Essays: Volume Two*, ed. Rachel Bowlby (London: Penguin, 1993), 43.

8   Donald T. Torchiana, *W. B. Yeats and Georgian Ireland* (Washington D.C.: The Catholic University of America Press, 1966), 123. Compare John Kelly's claim that Yeats in early April of 1930 "becomes obsessed by Swift, Bolingbroke and Pope." See Kelly, *A W. B. Yeats Chronology* (Basingstoke: Palgrave Macmillan, 2003), 268.

9   On the concept of "frustrators," see Yeats's account of the automatic writing sessions with his wife in *CW14* 10–13.

10   See for instance Peter Ure, *Yeats the Playwright: A Commentary on Character and Design in the Major Plays* (London: Routledge & Kegan Paul. 1963), 102–23.

11   Richard Taylor, *A Reader's Guide to the Plays of W. B. Yeats* (New York: St. Martin's Press, 1984), 132.

12   W. B. Yeats, *The Words upon the Window Pane: Manuscript Materials*, ed. Mary Fitzgerald (Ithaca, NY and London: Cornell University Press, 2002), 25–27.

13   A. S. Knowland, *W. B. Yeats: Dramatist of Vision* (Gerards Cross: Colin Smythe, 1983), 183.

14   See Robert E. Norton, *The Beautiful Soul: Aesthetic Morality in the Eighteenth Century* (Ithaca, NY and London: Cornell University Press, 1995).

15   Terence Brown, *The Life of W. B. Yeats: A Critical Biography* (Oxford: Blackwell, 2001), 331.

16   On this topic, see Charles I. Armstrong, "An 'Experiment in Living': Bohemianism and Homelessness in W. B. Yeats's *Autobiographies*," in eds. John Lynch and Katherina Dodou, *The Leaving of Ireland: Migration and Belonging in Irish Literature and Film* (Oxford: Peter Lang, 2015), 273–91.

17   R. F. Foster links both *The Only Jealousy of Emer* (which is the basis of *Fighting the Waves*) and *The Writing upon the Window-Pane* to the complex erotic entanglements Yeats's relationship to Iseult Gonne led him into. See Foster, *W. B. Yeats: A Life. II. The Arch-Poet, 1915–1939* (Oxford: Oxford University Press, 2003), 410, 109.

18   See George's letter dated November 24, 1931, and Yeats's response on November 25 (with an added note and comment), in *YGYL*, 270–72.

19   Yeats, *The Words upon the Window Pane: Manuscript Materials*, 95. Partially overlapping with "Pages from a Diary in 1930," the introduction also interprets Swift's *Discourse of the Contests and Dissensions between the Nobles and the Commons in Athens and Rome* in a way that makes it affirm, and conform to, the historical scheme of *A Vision*. For Swift's and this text's appearance in the latter, see *CW14* 36 and Margaret Mills Harper and Catherine E. Paul's editorial comment, 335 n39.

20   Matthew de Forrest, "Atemporal Presence of the Discarnate States of *A Vision* in *Words upon the Window Pane* and *Purgatory*," in *The Yeats Journal of Korea* 54 (Winter 2017), 168.

21   Thomas Hardy, *A Pair of Blue Eyes*, ed. with notes by Alan Manford (Oxford: Oxford University Press, 2005), 199.

22   Walter Benjamin, *Illuminations: Essays and Reflections*, ed. and intro. Hannah Arendt, trans. Harry Zohn (New York: Schocken, 1968), 263.

23   Louise Barnett, *Jonathan Swift in the Company of Women* (Oxford: Oxford University Press, 2007), 21.

24   Mary Fitzgerald, "Introduction," in Yeats, *The Words upon the Window Pane: Manuscript Materials*, xv–xxviii.

25   Florence Bell, *The Dean of St. Patrick's: A Play in Four Acts* (London: Edward Arnold, 1903), 63.

26   Michael McAteer, *Yeats and European Drama* (Cambridge: Cambridge University Press, 2010), 164.

27   Leo Damrosch, *Jonathan Swift: His Life and His World* (New Haven, CT and London: Yale University Press, 2013), 6–7.

28   Jonathan Swift, *Major Works*, ed. with intro. and notes, Angus Ross and David Woolley (Oxford: Oxford University Press, 1984), 522.

29   Swift, *Major Works*, 344.

30   Swift, *Major Works*, 351.

31   Swift, *Major Works*, 4.

32   Jonathan Swift, *Journal to Stella: Letters to Esther Johnson and Rebecca Dingley, 1710–1713*, ed. Abigail Williams (Cambridge: Cambridge University Press, 2013), 166–67.

33   See Harold Bloom, *The Anxiety of Influence: A Theory of Poetry*, 2nd edn. (New York: Oxford University Press, 1997), 70 and 152.

THE "ENDLESS DANCE OF CONTRAPUNTAL ENERGY": CONFLICT AND DISUNITY IN *FIGHTING THE WAVES*

Inés Bigot

Fighting the Waves,[1] the prose rewriting of *The Only Jealousy of Emer* (first published in 1919), stands as the perfect example of Yeats's achievements in the field of total theater, harmoniously blending orchestral music with dance, song, and spoken dialogue. Shortly after its first production, Yeats wrote enthusiastically to Olivia Shakespear with the news: "My *Fighting the Waves* has been my greatest success on the stage since *Kathleen-ni-Houlihan*." He declared the performance "a great event here, the politician[s] and the governor general and the American minister present," and he described key elements of the production—the masks designed "by the Dutchman [Hildo Van] Krop" and Georges Antheil's musical score—as "magnificent." By his own estimation, Yeats had finally realized his life-long search for a non-naturalistic kind of drama rooted in a subtle interaction among the multiple component media of the theatrical experience: "Everyone here is as convinced as I am that I have discovered a new form by this combination of dance, speech, and music" (*L* 768). Over the years, Yeats scholars have tended to agree.[2] Although *Fighting the Waves* is more often mentioned than analyzed in detail, the play is generally regarded as marking a departure from the minimalistic dramaturgy of the *Four Plays for Dancers*[3] in favor of a new, totalizing vision where music, voice, movement, and spectacle work together. As Pierre Longuenesse explains *Fighting the Waves* was conceived as an ambitious lyrical, choreographic, and orchestral performance that included six dancers and a solo dancer (Ninette de Valois), three lyrical singers and ten musicians, as well as Van Krop's masks and Dorothy Travers Smith's costumes, which added to the spectacular dimension.[4] Crucially, the play relies at its core on what Longuenesse calls "l'expressivité [...] de la danse [the expressive role of dance]."[5]

It is precisely the nature of the "expressive" role dance plays in this revised version of *The Only Jealousy of Emer* that is of primary interest here. Whereas the earlier version contained only one dance, *Fighting the Waves* frames that central dance with two others, thus creating a tripart structure that reflects Yeats's dramaturgical reinvestment in the expressive power of dancing bodies. The prologue takes the form of a choreographed battle meant to visually represent the Fool's speech at the close of *On Baile's Strand* and Emer's speech near the opening of *The Only Jealousy of Emer*, both of which describe Cuchulain's fight against the "deathless sea" (*CW2*, *Fighting the Waves*, 457) after discovering that the young man he has killed was his own son. The epilogue of *Fighting* the Waves is dedicated to Fand's own bitter dance and stands in sharp contrast to the preceding one, in which she uses her otherworldly charm in an effort to seduce the Ghost of Cuchulain.[6] Like the replacement of spoken accounts with spectacle at the outset, Yeats's decision to delete the verbal exchange between Fand and the Ghost of Cuchulain (which takes place during her dance in the original version), so that Ninette de Valois could play the now silent part, emphasizes his dedication to the dancer and, more generally, his renewed confidence in choreography. Far from being used as a simple adjunct to words, dance is a language of its own in *Fighting the Waves*. As Yeats himself suggested in the introduction to the play published in *Wheels and Butterflies*, dance, along with music and songs, is invested with a specific communicative potential: "I rewrote the play not only to fit it for such a stage [public stage] but to free it from abstraction and confusion. I have retold the story in prose which I have tried to make very simple, and left imaginative suggestion to dancers, singers, musicians."[7] Located (with)in the sphere of "imaginative suggestion," which probably points to the dancing body's ability to efficiently evoke intense experiences and truths that verbal language would only inappropriately grasp, dance is seen as being part and parcel of the playwright's attempt to clarify the plot and make it more accessible.

Indeed, in this play which hinges on a "resurrection ritual"[8] led by two women "struggling with the sea" (*CW2*, *Fighting the Waves*, 459)—Emer (Cuchulain's wife) and Eithne (Cuchulain's mistress)—the three dance episodes bring one of the main themes to the foreground, namely the conflictual relationship between the material and the supernatural worlds, the latter being embodied by Fand, the Woman of the Sidhe. The danced prologue which shows Cuchulain fighting the waves and being overpowered by them can of course be interpreted as a proof of his madness, as he mistakes the waves for his enemy, Conchubar. However, the battle also symbolically points to the dual relation humans have with the supernatural world—here, the country-under-wave which Emer and Eithne themselves are fighting as they try to save Cuchulain from the hold of Fand. The whole play bears witness to this relationship based on simultaneous attraction and rejection, an antagonistic interrelation that cannot give way to pure fusion, as Fand's two dances exemplify by registering her failure to unite with Cuchulain. All of this suggests that dance, in *Fighting the Waves*, is far removed from the image of "Unity of Being"[9] with which it tends to be associated in some of Yeats's poems and plays[10] and in much of the scholarship on these works.[11] Stemming from anger, unfulfilled desire, or bitterness, the dances record the impossibility of a true and lasting reconciliation between opposites, the unreachability of unity and uniformity.

In this article, I engage with the paradoxical emphasis on the themes of conflict, discord, and dis-unity in a play which is nonetheless often regarded as an example of total theater, a form which implies the alliance and coexistence, albeit not always the complete fusion, of the different media involved. I view the three dances as comments on these notions which lie at the core of *Fighting the Waves*, embodied by the disabled spirit of the Sidhe, Bricriu—Fand's enemy and self-proclaimed "maker of discord" who has possessed Cuchulain's body since his fight with the waves. Far from representing some kind of idealized mode of being or symbolizing a model for collective harmony, the dances confront us with lonely individuals who experience, through their moving bodies, a new-found, self-reliant identity. In this reading, the function of dancing bodies is analogous to that of masks in the 1937 version of *A Vision*, in the sense that "Yeats's last Masks," as Margaret Mills Harper usefully notes, "are multiple rather than one side of a duality (of self and anti-self)" and are not meant to "stress [...] unity though they recognize that yearning for [unity] drives life."[12] I contend that the emphasis on defeat or dis-unity in the dances, and more generally speaking in the whole play,[13] is not to be taken as a negative, pessimistic comment on the imperfection of human beings and bodies. Rather, this late play evidences Yeats's more open conception of identity, one that is metamorphic, fluid, embodied, and constructed through the confrontation, interaction, and negotiation with alterity—what Harper describes as the "endless dance of contrapuntal energy."[14]

I begin with an analysis of the silent but eloquent discourse delivered by the dances in order to enhance their "imaginative suggestion" of the play's pivotal theme: the ambiguous relationship between the human and the supernatural realms. I then reflect on Bricriu's two-fold role in the action as the "maker of discord," following Ken Monteith's insightful reevaluation of the disabled character.[15] I argue that Bricriu's intervention—"helping" Emer to save the Ghost of Cuchulain from the hold of Fand on the condition that she renounce her husband's love—marks the start of a process of emancipation for Emer and Fand. This feminist reading of *Fighting the Waves* is grounded in the specific context of a play which features an unusually weakened, passive, unheroic Cuchulain whose life depends on Emer's decision.[16] It also ties in with Yeats's subtle exploration of the themes of feminine liberation and "self-reliance" in his drama where the "manful energy" (VP 849) he was seeking is often faced with a dissident womanly strength, from *The Land of Heart's Desire* (1894) to the rewritings of the Salomé biblical episode *The King of the Great Clock Tower* (1934) and *A Full Moon in March* (1935).[17]

Fighting the Waves was Yeats and de Valois's first collaborative project. After meeting in Cambridge in 1927, Yeats asked de Valois to help him create the Abbey School of Ballet[18] (1927–1933) and to work on revivals of several dance plays, including *At the Hawk's Well* (staged in 1933) and *The King of the Great Clock Tower* (1934). As de Valois explains in *Come Dance with Me*, by collaborating with her, Yeats was hoping to bring back to life "the poetic drama of Ireland."[19] Born Edris Stannus in Ireland (County Wicklow) and considered to be the founder of British ballet, de Valois was the ideal dancer for Yeats, considering her rich and eclectic background. Her experience in the Ballets Russes, founded by the Russian art critic and arts patron Serge Diaghilev, had taught her to think of dance as an integrated art form within a larger theatrical frame that combined design, movement, and music: "the main effect of Diaghilev on my dormant mind," she wrote, "was to arouse an intense interest in the ballet in relation to the theatre. I further sensed its own singular position in the theatre."[20] Her work as choreographic director at the Festival Theatre in Cambridge led by her cousin, Terence Gray, strengthened her knowledge of non-naturalistic total theater staging techniques, since Gray advocated symbolic and expressionist productions reliant on masks and stylized gesture.[21] Consequently, the dancer seemed perfectly capable of helping Yeats to create through symbolic dances what Richard Allen Cave terms "embodied poetry."[22] De Valois herself describes her dances in Yeats's plays as "modern" and "stylized":

> That is, modern in the way that classical dancers can move in any style they want. I used movement that was highly stylized. The dances were very abstract—masked you couldn't be anything else, anything would have been out of place. One really did use the simplest gestures possible, rather symbolic movements, really, one avoided the more full-blooded realistic theater.[23]

The fact that de Valois's dances were abstract and symbolic doesn't mean that they were disembodied. We will see later on that Fand's first dance is erotic as well as ethereal.

As noted earlier, the dance of seduction in *The Only Jealousy of Emer* features a verbal exchange between Fand and the Ghost of Cuchulain that Yeats omits in the new prose version. This was partly because de Valois refused to speak on stage; but the silence of the dancer also corresponds to a specific state of being, one of remoteness and aloofness that suited the mysterious roles she played in works such as *At the Hawk's Well* and *The King of the Great Clock Tower*. As Cave notes, "It would seem that her chosen technique for performing these roles endorsed this somewhat remote quality of being; to have joined with the other actors in the pieces through the medium of speech would have robbed her of this distinctive separateness."[24] What stands out from these comments is the "separateness" of the dancer who does not use the same expressive medium as the other actors.

However, Yeats's plays do not dramatize the dancing body as a mere nonsensical oddity; instead they invest it with meaningful power. *In Fighting the Waves*, the dancing bodies are "speaking bodies," to quote an expression Frank Kermode uses in *Romantic Image* when discussing the figure of the dancer in a Yeatsian poetic context.[25] In this play, as in other late plays such as *A Full Moon in March* (1935) and *The Death of Cuchulain* (1939), dance is presented as a language in its own right, acquiring a distinctive, potent role in the narrative of the fable and the expression of the characters' inner feelings. Yeats resorts to dance several times in *Fighting the Waves* as a significant "discursive silence,"[26] a bodily language combining "showing" with "telling."

Before looking closely at the dances, let us explain briefly what we mean by using the expression "discursive silence," which is borrowed from Arnaud Ryner.[27] As Sylvia Ellis shows in *The Plays of W. B. Yeats: Yeats and the Dancer*, the question of the relationship between language and dance has been explored at length by philosophers and theoreticians. Although one can draw a parallel between language and dance, to the extent that both constitute "symbolic systems," the latter does not share all the characteristics of language, among which Ellis mentions synonymity and translatability.[28] My purpose therefore is not to prove that dance is an exact equivalent to verbal language but to stress Yeats's acute awareness of the unique power of bodily expression on stage. Far from being limited to an undecipherable primitive action, dance is invested with complex symbolic meaning in *Fighting the Waves*.[29] Hence, the detailed, even eloquent stage directions accompanying each dance:

These dances form in themselves a tryptic, a significant "text" that can be "read" when analyzed in the context of a play that focuses on Emer and Eithne Inguba's attempt to bring back to life the inanimate hero Cuchulain. The two women's fight against the supernatural world of the country-under-wave is foreshadowed by the choreographed prologue (first dance): "*A man wearing the Cuchulain mask enters from one side with sword and shield. He dances a dance which represents a man fighting the waves.*" (*CW2, Fighting the Waves*, 455). Choosing to embody on the stage what was only reported through Emer's words in *The Only Jealousy of Emer* allows the audience to more intimately access the event as they are able to witness Cuchulain's fight and subsequent defeat directly.[30] His mesmerizing and mesmerized "*cataleptic stare upon some distant imaginary object*" at the end of the dance anticipates his encounter with Fand and already captures the impossible union between the material world and the distant supernatural country-under-wave. Here, Cuchulain's personal experience acquires a universal value; it points out, in language from *A Vision*, that if "life is an endeavor made vain by the four sails of its mill" then "all the gains of man come from conflict with the opposite of his true being" (*AVB* 70, 11).

In the second dance, Yeats once again entirely confides in the strength of the dancer's ability to embody feelings and human experiences that lie beyond the reach of verbal language. Fand's seductive dance, which is meant to be self-explanatory, is not accompanied by any verbal account for her behavior, as was the case in the preceding play, *The Only Jealousy of Emer*, where she clearly stated the stakes of the dance: "Because I long I am not complete" (*CW2* 325); "Time shall seem to stay its course; / When your mouth and my mouth meet / All my round shall be complete / Imagining all its circles run; / And there shall be oblivion / Even to quench Cuchulain's drouth, / Even to still that heart" (326). Fand, who is described by the Ghost of Cuchulain as "shedding such light from limb and hair / As when the moon, complete at last / With every laboring crescent past, / And lonely with extreme delight, / Flings out upon the fifteenth night?" (325), is nonetheless incomplete since she still needs to coexist with her opposite, Cuchulain, in order to reach that state of Unity of Being represented by the full moon. Her search for such unity takes the form of a dance which she uses to coax Cuchulain into following her to the country-under-wave. The dance contains the very duality mentioned previously when discussing the ambiguous relationship between the mortal and the supernatural worlds, as Fand is simultaneously alluring—"*Fand, moves round the crouching Ghost of Cuchulain [...]. At moments, she may drop her hair upon his head*"— and distant—"*but she does not kiss him*" (*CW2, Fighting the Waves*, 461). The last stage direction describing her dance prepares us for Fand and Cuchulain's failure to reach Unity of Being: "*The object of the dance is that having awakened Cuchulain he will follow Fand out; probably he will seek a kiss and the kiss will be withheld*" (461). Fand's dance thus puts forward the idea that the building up of individual identity implies interaction and confrontation with alterity, no matter how the strife ends.

On the night of the first performance of *Fighting the Waves* at the Abbey Theatre, George Antheil's provocative music added to the discordant dimension of a dance which does not lead to union. The American composer chose to "eschew all melodic or harmonic interest" in favor of a musical accompaniment which illustrated the "overwhelming turbulence"[31] of the duel between the mortal world and the supernatural one through the use of variations in pitch. Theater critic Joseph Holloway was unimpressed, acerbically declaring that "the steam whistle organ or a merry-go-round discourses heavenly music by comparison with the music shook out of a bag of notes anyhow by the American concoctor of this riot of discords."[32] Yet it is precisely this element of discord that made Antheil's score so appropriate for a play in which dissonance and dis-unity prevail.

In his reading of *Fighting the Waves*, Cave mentions the existence of a holograph manuscript containing the following stage direction at the point in the action where Fand's first dance occurs: "*They dance.*" He argues that the plural "they" leads us to reconsider the nature of the relationship between Cuchulain and Fand. Whereas Cuchulain is supposed to remain in a crouching posture during this scene in *The Only Jealousy of Emer*, this particular holograph manuscript of *Fighting the Waves* suggests that "Cuchulain's Ghost is responsive to the lure of the dance and physically commits himself to Fand's medium of expression through the body."[33] The emotional and bodily impact of Fand on Cuchulain is thus heightened and the "potential for union"[34] is stressed:

> Where in the first version the stage picture intimated Fand's defeat from the moment of her appearance, what is evoked in this revised version simply by the addition of that plural pronoun, "they," is the possibility of Cuchulain's succumbing to Fand's power and her magnetism as expressed through the dance.[35]

Since the final published version of *Fighting the Waves* does not contain this stage direction and only mentions Fand's dance, one is tempted to conclude that Yeats ultimately chose to insist on the predicted difficulty of a fusion between Fand and Cuchulain. However, although Cuchulain's immobility is mentioned at the beginning, there is no written element in the text that suggests he remains in a crouching position; on the contrary, the following stage direction indicates that he has gotten up: "*Fand and Cuchulain go out*" (*CW2, Fighting the Waves*, 463). Let us not forget that the Ghost of Cuchulain was played by a dancer, Hedley Briggs, in the 1929 production at the Abbey Theatre.[36] A staging of the play which would present the dance as a duet would then be relevant considering the stakes of the scene. The staging could either choose to stress the "potential for union" between the two characters mentioned by Cave or, more convincingly, present the duet as a duel, which is what Melinda Szüts did in her own production of *The Only Jealousy of Emer* at the O'Donoghue Theatre in Galway in May 2018.[37] Here, Fand's hypnotic dance quickly turns into an adversarial *pas de deux* between a stumbling Cuchulain, erotically attracted to Fand, and the dancer, who alternates between movements suggestive of seduction and a readiness to flee. The choreography brings to the foreground the unreachable quality of Fand, whom Cuchulain follows without being able to stop, as well as Fand's final defeat as Cuchulain resists the temptation of kissing her after Emer's sacrificial decision.

Fand's "bitterness" (*CW2, Fighting the Waves*, 463) is fully expressed in her last dance, eloquently called, "Fand mourns among the waves" (463) and echoing the First Musician's song in which the "bitter reward / Of many a tragic tomb!" is already mentioned. Her "final pose of despair" (463) reminds us of Cuchulain's own motionless stance at the end of the prologue, apparently enhancing her overthrow and loneliness. Once again, on the opening night at the Abbey Theatre in 1929, Antheil's music illustrated Fand's failure to reach fusion with her opposite by offsetting "a high-pitched melody with a low, tremulous accompaniment."[38] The sudden "surges of urgent rhythmic chord-effects"[39] which interrupted the accompaniment contributed to stress Fand's unappeased desire. However, the "statue of solitude" (*CW2, Fighting the Waves*, 462) to which the First Musician alludes not only mirrors Fand's situation but also Emer's who has renounced Cuchulain's love and the possibility of sitting by the fire with him again.[40]

Disunity, separation, and sadness thus seem to prevail after Bricriu's intervention, relegating both women to the margins of Cuchulain's life. The spirit of the Sidhe indeed explains his intention to divide and rule right from the start in response to Emer's question "Come for what purpose?" when he asserts that he "shows [his] face and everything he [Cuchulain] loves must fly" (*CW2, Fighting the Waves*, 460). Later in the play, he adds, "I am Fand's enemy. I come to tell you how to thwart her" (462). Despite the blurriness of his true purpose, the character's stance as a "maker of discord" (460) is striking. The real question revolves around the consequences of such a will to counter harmony and wreak havoc on the various characters' well-thought-out plans. I would argue, following Monteith's lead, that whatever dark feelings might account for Bricriu's antagonistic attitude, the consequence of his intervention is not to be interpreted in exclusively negative terms. As Monteith suggests, Emer's act of renunciation and sacrifice invests her with heroic stature paving the way for a life of self-reliance and wisdom.[41] She is more active than her own supposedly masculine husband Cuchulain, who is nothing but the object of the three women's desire and love in this play.[42]

As for the character of Fand, her defeat and disappointment are offset by the hypnotic quality of her dance, which steals the show at the end of *Fighting the Waves*—her "pose of despair" possibly evoking a certain degree of pride and awareness of the power of her body. Alone on the stage[43] since the "wave curtain" has been drawn by the Musicians "*until it masks the bed, Cuchulain, Eithne Inguba, and Emer*" (*CW2, Fighting the Waves*, 462), she definitely has the "last word" even though she is now "trapped within the smaller confines of the forestage formed by the painted drop curtain and by the formation of the 'waves,'" and her movements no longer share "the expansiveness of her earlier dance, which darted into all the available space offered by the full stage."[44] Bearing in mind the reversal of traditional gender roles mentioned earlier, one could qualify Cave's take on the last dance which leads him to see Fand's decreased "vitality"[45] as proof of the "loss of her self-possession, control of space, her joy in the body."[46] Locating Fand's dance within Yeats's exploration of the theme of feminine "self-reliance" in this play implies reading it as a step forward in the character's difficult process of emancipation. What's more,

Fand's captivating first dance cannot be forgotten so quickly. It lingers in the readers and the spectators' mind, as Moore's remarks on the play demonstrate:

> I saw your *Fighting with the Waves* at Hammersmith[47] and greatly enjoyed it. The masks though needlessly grotesque were full of imagination and very effective. [...] But the great moment was the entrance and dance of Fand and her mask; even her costume though funny, was far the best (*TSMC* 161).

Considering the fact that de Valois played the role in what Cave describes as a bold, sensual, courageous manner, Fand's dances acquire a whole new dimension as they point to female liberation through the body. Cave's comments on Fand's first dance are particularly helpful when it comes to identifying the erotically charged quality of de Valois's transgressive choreography, which suggests the dancer's "*difference*, as one who lives in and through the body:"

> For its time in Ireland this was a courageous, politically subversive stance for a female performer of Irish descent to adopt or, more importantly, to *embody*. Though de Valois's body is fully clothed, it is fearlessly displayed and open, derisive of the gaze and judgement of everyone on stage who is watching her (and by implication of the audience in the theatre too).[48]

Cave bases his argument on a surviving photograph from the Abbey Theatre production, showing de Valois "with arms and head flung back in a derisive challenge as Emer threatens her with a knife."[49] This shows that Fand's bodily appropriation of stage space during her first dance underlines her power and self-asserting identity *before* she even tries to reach Unity of Being. The openness of Valois's body and her "forward-thrusting pelvis" lead to a "deployment of her whole body" which strongly contrasts with "Emer's stilted, arrested movement" and the "cowering figure of Cuchulain."[50] In addition, de Valois's choreography recalls Isadora Duncan's own technique—based on the use of the pelvis and the solar plexus—as described by Elizabeth Anderson:

> Duncan's technique situates movement and energy as originating with the breath and in the body's inner core—the pelvis and solar plexus—and flowing outward to radiate from the limbs, pervading the performance space. The dancer's body is extended, open, in process.[51]

Taking as a starting point Ann Daly's comments on Duncan's movements which interpret the dance as a "process," as being about "becoming a self (the subject-in-process/on trial) rather than about displaying a body,"[52] Anderson argues that "Duncan's work is about becoming a self in the very activity of displaying (the moving) body."[53] Even though de Valois was a classically trained dancer, we know that she danced with bare feet in Yeats's plays and in an abstract manner that she herself called "modern."[54] Bearing in mind the links between Yeats's vision of the dance and early modern dancers' work—and more specifically Duncan's—it is interesting to read Fand's dances in the light of this phenomenon of "becoming a self."[55]

Bricriu's interference keeps Fand from reaching Unity of Being, which means that she will still be driven by that "longing" she mentions in *The Only Jealousy of Emer*, a form of desire that proves she is not "complete" yet: "Because I long I am not complete" (*CW2* 325).[56] But this imperfection she laments in the last dance is precisely what makes her more human than she seemed to be in her first dance, where she is described as an artefact, a being from an otherworldly dimension: "*Her mask and clothes must suggest gold or bronze or brass and silver, so that she seems more an idol than a human being. This suggestion may be repeated in her movements. Her hair, too, must keep the metallic suggestion*" (*CW2, Fighting the Waves*, 461). The very impossibility of reaching that state of oblivion and stillness she describes in *The Only Jealousy of Emer* is what makes her "all woman" (*CW2*, 326). By depicting Fand as a full-blooded supernatural figure, Yeats eschews the stereotypical, idealized vision of women as pure, ethereal goddesses without yielding to the easy temptation of over-sexualizing and demonizing the dancer.

Ironically Bricriu's plan, which could be interpreted as purely evil, results in a process of liberation for both Emer and Fand, who are ultimately confronted by their own selves and bodies after losing the opportunity to possess Cuchulain's own "feminized" body.[57] Released of their "own jealousy," Emer and Fand are thus implicitly invited to work towards mental and bodily self-possession, however painful and imperfect a perspective this may be. Emer does not dance in this play but she will after her husband's death in *The Death of Cuchulain* (1939), which I read as a proof of the incremental process of the character's physical emancipation. Emer's dance is all the more representative of an inner shift since it is her only apparition in *The Death of Cuchulain*: doomed to be separated from her husband after her heroic renunciation, she gives full vent to her deepest feelings in this dance around the severed heads of Cuchulain's enemies, watching over her dead husband's reincarnation as a bird:

In *Fighting the Waves*, as in this last play of the Cuchulain cycle,[58] the dance mediates a discourse on bodily identity which differs from that conveyed in other late plays such as *The King of the Great Clock Tower* (1934) or its rewriting, *A Full Moon in March* (1935). In the latter plays, the dance ultimately leads to a form of Unity of Being through the fusion of the opposites that the Queen and the Stroller (*The King and the Great Clock Tower*) and the Queen and the Swineherd (*A Full Moon in March*) stand for. On the contrary, in *Fighting the Waves*, Yeats explores the failure of communion and unity, confronting us with characters (dancing or not) who experience bodily separation from their counterparts and are faced with the necessary imperfection of the material sphere.

Throughout the play, the spatialization of the characters' bodies points to the impossibility of coexisting in the same place. As Alexandra Poulain shows in her article on *The Only Jealousy of Emer*, the "whole point of the tragedy is in fact linked to Cuchulain's irreducible absence, and to Emer's failure to bring him back into the dramatic space (the space where characters meet, talk together and interact), which is to say in their house where the play is set."[59] As discussed earlier, Fand and Cuchulain cannot unite either, and the kiss which is supposed to seal their reunion never takes place: "*probably he will seek a kiss and the kiss will be withheld*" (*CW2, Fighting the Waves*, 461).

It is particularly significant that "the maker of discord," Bricriu, characterized by his withered hand, should take bodily possession of "heroic" Cuchulain and be invested with the power of thwarting his temptation to live with Fand "in Mananann's house" as "the gods who remember nothing" (*CW2, Fighting the Waves*, 461). As a physical example of deformity and bodily incompleteness, Bricriu, albeit a spirit from the sea, triggers the sequence of events that will lead to Cuchulain's return to the living, material world, far from the ideal, statue-like beauty from which he ultimately turns "his too human breast" (463). Consequently, Cuchulain's recovery of "his own rightful form" (462) at the end must not hide the underlying discourse on identity and the body that runs throughout the play: embracing an open view of physicality, *Fighting the Waves* comes to terms with the inevitably flawed but nonetheless powerful realm of the body, enriching a stream of thought that pervades Yeats's drama.

NOTES

1   The play was published in 1934 in W. B. Yeats, *Wheels and Butterflies* (London: Macmillan, 1934). It was presented at the Abbey Theatre on August 13, 1929 by the National Theatre Society, Ltd., with the following cast: Michael J. Dolan (Cuchulain); Meriel Moore (Emer); Shelah Richards (Eithne Inguba); Ninette de Valois (Fand); J. Stephenson (Singer); Hedley Briggs (Ghost of Cuchulain); Chris Sheehan, Mai Kiernan, Cepta Cullen, Doreen Cuthbert, Margaret Horgan, and Thelma Murphy (Waves). It was produced by Lennox Robinson with music by George Antheil and choreography by Ninette de Valois (*CW2* 899).

2   See Pierre Longuenesse, *Yeats et la scène. L'acteur et sa voix à l'Abbey Theatre de Dublin* (Villeneuve d'Ascq: Presses Universitaires du Septentrion, 2015), 139–50; Longuenesse, "Le 'regard aveugle' dans le théâtre de W. B. Yeats," *Études théâtrales* 2, no. 65 (2016), 79–93; Mary Fleischer, *Embodied Texts: Symbolist Playwright-Dancer Collaborations* (Amsterdam: Rodopi, 2007), 233–49; and Richard Allen Cave, *Collaborations: Ninette de Valois and William Butler Yeats* (Alton: Dance Books Ltd, 2011), 47–70.

3   *At the Hawk's Well* (1917), *The Dreaming of the Bones* (1919), *The Only Jealousy of Emer* (1919), *Calvary* (1920).

4   Longuenesse, *Yeats et la scène*, 144–47.

5   Longuenesse, *Yeats et la scène*, 147.

6   In the list of the "Persons in the Play," the use of three different names to refer to Emer's husband is striking: Cuchulain, the Ghost of Cuchulain (who interacts with Fand and whom Emer is able to see thanks to Bricriu), and the Figure of Cuchulain (Bricriu).

7   Yeats, *Wheels and Butterflies*, 69.

8   I borrow this expression from Jacqueline Genet, *Le théâtre de William Butler Yeats* (Villeneuve-d'Ascq: Presses universitaires du Septentrion, 1995), 243.

9   As James Flannery explains: "by the term Unity of Being Yeats summed up many of his ideas on the ideal state of the human personality […]. He equated Unity of Being with 'the thinking of the body' and compared it to the art of Dante in subordinating 'all parts to the whole as in a perfectly proportioned human body.'" Flannery, *W. B. Yeats and the Idea of a Theatre. The Early Abbey Theatre in Theory and Practice* (New Haven, CT and London: Yale University Press, 1976), 58–59. In *A Vision*, Yeats says that the Unity of Being of Phase Fifteen belongs to a different order of existence where conflicts and strife, which characterize human experience, are absent: "Phase 1 and Phase 15 are not human incarnations because human life is impossible without strife between the *tinctures*" (*AVB* 59).

10   I'm thinking of poems such as "The Double Vision of Michael Robartes" (1919) or "Among School Children" (1928), and of plays such as *The Cat and the Moon* (1917), *The King of the Great Clock Tower* (1934), or *A Full Moon in March* (1935).

11   See, for example, Frank Kermode, *Romantic Image* [1957] Electronic edition, Taylor and Francis e-Library, 2004), 59–123. See also Genet, "Dance in Yeats's Plays: A Quest for Unity," *Études anglaises* 4, vol. 68 (2015): 397–410.

12   Margaret Mills Harper, "*A Vision* and Yeats's Late Masks," in YA19, eds. Margaret Mills Harper and Warwick Gould (Cambridge: Open Book Publishers, 2013), 163.

13   Emer, who does not dance, is made to renounce her only hope to share a private space with her husband, Cuchulain; see Alexandra Poulain, "'Westward Ho!': *The Only Jealousy of Emer*, From Noh to Tragedy," in *Writing Modern Ireland*, ed. Catherine E. Paul (Clemson, SC: Clemson University Press, 2015), 95–103. Bricriu, whose deformed body reflects his will to sow the seeds of discord among the characters, has come to thwart Fand, who comes from the same world as he.

14   This expression was used by Margaret Mills Harper in the conclusion to her paper "*Wheels and Butterflies* as Comedy," delivered at the International Yeats Society Symposium, December 15–16, 2018, Kyoto, Japan.

15   See Ken Monteith's reading of *The Only Jealousy of Emer* "from a disability studies perspective" in "Enabling Emer, Disabling the Sidhe: W. B. Yeats's *The Only Jealousy of Emer*," in *Writing Modern Ireland*, ed. Catherine E. Paul (Clemson, SC: Clemson University Press, 2015), 99–110.

16   Monteith underlines the "comatose-like state" (101) of "the Irish hero of the Ulster cycle," renowned for "his great strength and battle rage [which] set him apart from other warriors" (100) in "Enabling Emer, Disabling the Sidhe." His re-evaluation of Bricriu's critical role in the play leads him to interpret Emer's situation in terms of "sacrifice" but also of "self-reliance," a notion that I bear in mind while analyzing Fand's dances in *Fighting the Waves*. My reading thus runs counter to the idea that Bricriu's action is in favor of the status quo, as expressed by Amy Koritz: "a faithful wife silently sacrificing herself for an adulterous husband […], and a male hero around whose fate revolves all the action—and all the women. Finally, the narrative presents the dominance of a male god over a female

counterpart." Amy Koritz, "Women Dancing: The Structure of Gender in Yeats's Early Plays for Dancers," *Modern Drama* 32, no. 3 (Fall 1989), 393.

17 In these two plays, the Queen's need to reach Unity of Being through sexual fusion with her opposite (the stroller; the swineherd) would seem to suggest her dependence on a male figure. But the simultaneously erotic and castrating dance with the severed head invests her with self-assertive gestural values that reconfigure the existing balance of power.

18 For more details on Ninette de Valois and the Abbey School of Ballet, see Victoria O' Brien, *A History of Irish Ballet from 1927 to 1963* (Bern: Peter Lang, 2011), and Deirdre Mulrooney, *Irish Moves: An Illustrated History of Dance and Physical Theatre in Ireland* (Dublin: The Liffey Press, 2006).

19 Ninette de Valois, *Come Dance with Me* (Cleveland, OH: The World Publishing Company, 1957), 104.

20 De Valois, *Come Dance with Me*, 88.

21 See Fleischer, *Embodied Texts*, 228–29, and Cave, *Collaborations*.

22 Cave, *Collaborations*, xvi.

23 G. M. Pinciss, "A Dancer for Mr. Yeats," *Educational Theatre Journal* 21, no. 4 (1969): 389.

24 Cave, *Collaborations*, 47.

25 Kermode, *Romantic Image*, 69.

26 I borrow this expression, "la pantomime comme silence discursif, " from Arnaud Rykner, *L'envers du théâtre: dramaturgie du silence de l'âge classique à Maeterlinck* (Paris: Corti, 1996), 214.

27 Arnaud Ryner, *L'envers du théâtre: dramaturgie due silence de l'âge Classique à Maerterlink* (Paris: Corti, 1996), 214.

28 Sylvia Ellis, *The Plays of W. B. Yeats: Yeats and the Dancer* (London: Macmillan, 1999), 248–50. Such comments have already been developed in two articles of mine, "De l'envers des mots au discours muet: danse et langage dans le théâtre de William Butler Yeats et de Wole Soyinka," *Recherches en danse*, "Focus," (Jul 2019), and "Dance and Dissidence in Wole Soyinka's Plays: From Status Quo to Revolution," *Commonwealth Essays and Studies* 42, no. 1 (2019).

29 For more details on the relationship between language, literature, and dance in an Irish theatrical context, see Katarzyna Ojrzynska, '*Dancing as if Language No Longer Existed*': *Dance in Contemporary Irish Drama* (Oxford: Peter Lang, 2014), and Bernadette Sweeney, *Performing the Body in Irish Theatre* (Basingstoke: Palgrave Macmillan, 2008). On the more general subject of the relationship between literature and dance in the modernist period, see Susan Jones, *Literature, Modernism, and Dance* (Oxford: Oxford University Press, 2013).

30 Here, I agree with Longuenesse's reading of the dance moments in his analysis of the play. See *Yeats et la scène*, 145.

31 Cave, *Collaborations*, 64.

32 Ellis, *The Plays of W. B. Yeats*, 329.

33 Cave, *Collaborations*, 52.

34 Cave, *Collaborations*, 52.

35 Cave, *Collaborations*, 52.

36 Briggs was an accomplished dancer who had collaborated with de Valois at the Cambridge Festival Theatre. Cave, *Collaborations*, 53.

37 The play, directed by Melinda Szüts, was performed by DancePlayers company, "a Galway-based ensemble of professional theater makers and musicians who produce collaborative pieces for physical theatre." See DancePlayers, "About," Facebook, accessed February 10, 2021, https://www.facebook.com/DancePlayersCompany/about/

38 Cave, *Collaborations*, 66.

39 Cave, *Collaborations*, 66.

40   See Alexandra Poulain, "'Westward Ho!,'" 98: "Their [the Musicians'] famously enigmatic
      final song seems to evoke the destiny of Fand, a 'statue of solitude,' an ideal of feminine
      beauty first beheld then forsaken by a fickle-hearted man. Yet the refrain 'O bitter reward
      / Of many a tragic tomb' also points towards Emer, a tragic heroine whose renouncement
      means a kind of death—a theatrical death at least canceling her out as a character and
      confining her to a purely choric function."
41   In Monteith's words, "As a result of her [Emer's] interaction with Bricriu, Yeats would have
      his audience believe that the character remains true to the 'pure flame that burns in her
      always,' that Yeats encountered in reading Lady Gregory's *Cuchulain of Muirthemne* (Ex
      332). While Yeats may want to celebrate Emer's noble sacrifice as evidence of her 'pure
      flame,' another outcome of her encounter with Bricriu is that she must become self-reliant."
      "Enabling Emer, Disabling the Sidhe," 105.
42   This is why I agree with Alexandra Poulain's reading of *The Only Jealousy of Emer*: "Cuchulain,
      the arch-hero, is entirely passive and remote, and is only displayed, paradoxically, as an
      absent character;" "'Westward Ho!,'" 91. Poulain notes that biographical readings which
      underline the parallels between Cuchulain's "tragic dilemma"—as he is torn between Emer,
      Eithne, and Fand—and Yeats's situation while writing *The Only Jealousy of Emer*—torn
      between George, Iseult Gonne, and Maud Gonne—focus on Cuchulain's own fate whereas
      this particular play hinges on Emer's decision. See "'Westward Ho!,'" 91.
43   She is alone, except from the presence of the anonymous "waves": "As before there may be
      other dancers who represent the waves" (*CW2* 463).
44   Cave, *Collaborations*, 66.
45   Cave, *Collaborations*, 66.
46   Cave, *Collaborations*, 67.
47   *Fighting the Waves* was indeed revived by De Valois on March 28, 1930 at the Lyric Theatre
      Hammersmith with identical cast and designs (see Fleischer, *Embodied Texts*, 245.)
48   Cave, *Collaborations*, 59. Emphasis in the original.
49   Cave, *Collaborations*, 59.
50   Cave, *Collaborations*, 59.
51   Elizabeth Anderson, "Dancing Modernism: Ritual, Ecstasy and the Female Body," *Literature
      and Theology* 22, no. 3 (2008): 358.
52   Ann Daly, "Dance History and Feminist Theory: Reconsidering Isadora Duncan and the
      Male Gaze," in *Gender and Performance: The Presentation of Difference in the Performing
      Arts*, ed. Lawrence Senelick (Hanover, NH: University Press of New England, 1992), 253.
53   Elizabeth Anderson, "Dancing Modernism," 358.
54   See Pinciss, "A Dancer for Mr. Yeats," 389.
55   On the influence of modern dance on Yeats's approach, see Ellis's *The Plays of W. B. Yeats*,
      in which she talks about the playwright's admiration for Loïe Fuller (160–62) and the
      connection between his conception of the dance and Isadora Duncan's (195–96).
56   In *A Vision*, Yeats explains that Phase 15, corresponding to Unity of Being, is the only one
      where "Thought and will are indistinguishable, effort and attainment are indistinguishable
      [...] where "love knows nothing of desire, for desire implies effort [...]" (AVB 101).
57   Ken Monteith, "Enabling Emer, Disabling the Sidhe," 103.
58   *On Baile's Strand* (1904), *The Green Helmet* (1910), *At the Hawk's Well* (1917), *The Only
      Jealousy of Emer* (1919), *The Death of Cuchulain* (1939).
59   Poulain, "'Westward Ho!,'" 91.

'[...] BUT A PLAY': LAUGHTER AND THE REINVENTION OF THEATER IN *THE RESURRECTION*

Alexandra Poulain

For anyone familiar with Yeats's earlier *Plays for Dancers*, inspired by—but not strictly imitative of—the Japanese tradition of Noh theater, *The Resurrection*[1] at first seems to present a familiar pattern. In the 1931 version, the inaugural stage direction makes the point explicitly that the play, originally intended for "*an ordinary stage*," was rewritten to fit the earlier pattern: "*I now changed the stage directions and wrote songs for the unfolding and folding of the curtain that it might be played in a studio or a drawing-room like my dance plays, or at the Peacock Theatre before a specially chosen audience*" (*CW2* 481). As Pierre Longuenesse[2] points out, the stage direction thus untypically becomes the site of a metacritical reflection where the playwright, speaking in the first person, reflects on the revision process through which he brought the play closer to the formal pattern of the original dance plays. We recognize the three Musicians, mediating between the actors and the audience, and the framing lyrics which accompany "*the folding and unfolding of the curtain*," in lieu of the painted cloth which featured in the earlier plays. More importantly, *The Resurrection* is based on one fundamental principle which the *Plays for Dancers* had borrowed from Noh dramaturgy: the fact that the action revolves on the encounter between two different, incongruent planes of reality—the everyday, commonplace reality of human experience and the spiritual reality of the Otherworld, embodied by ghosts, fairies or divine beings.

For all that familiar appearance, *The Resurrection* has long perplexed critics who puzzle over its real meaning. Is it a pagan or a Christian play? Is it really a theological play, or an allegory of "the creative imagination," as Helen Vendler suggests?[3] In a recent extensive reading of the play, Charles I. Armstrong astutely picks up Harold Bloom's comment that "the play hesitates on the threshold of Christianity"[4] and points out that the threshold is a crucial element of the spatial dramaturgy of the play, where the protagonists "keep vigil on a threshold, so as to hold out the outside masses." "Of course," he adds, "the followers' attempt to keep the mob outside is impotent: they cannot ward off the miraculous entry of Christ."[5] Armstrong additionally notes the formal similarity between *The Resurrection* and *The King's Threshold*, both set in a liminal space (from the Latin *limen*: threshold); but of course his comment implicitly makes the point that the literal threshold on which *The Resurrection* is set doubles as (and materializes) the metaphorical, porous threshold between World and Otherworld through which Christ passes, in keeping with the dramaturgical framework of all the dance plays. In this essay I continue to explore the implications of liminality in the play, which I read, in the wake of Helen Vendler, less as a theological play than as a meditation on artistic practice. More precisely, I read the play as an attempt to define what constitutes a competent spectator for Yeats's brand of experimental theater, and suggest that its quest for the ideal spectator hinges on its completely unconventional use of laughter (understood here as an event which occurs in the play rather than a reaction the play might elicit in the audience).

I am encouraged to read the play as a meditation on spectatorship by the opening lyric, which starts:

> I saw a staring virgin stand
> Where holy Dionysus died,
> And tear the heart out of his side,
> And lay the heart upon her hand
> And bear that beating heart away;
> And then did all the Muses sing
> Of Magnus Annus at the spring,
> As though God's death were but a play (*CW2* 481).

As Longuenesse observes, the song is not attributed to any specific speaker (unlike in the *Plays for Dancers* where the framing lyrics are attributed to the First Musician). The first words, "I saw," echo the inaugural stage direction ("Before I had finished this play I saw that its subject-matter might make it unsuited for the public stage," *CW2* 481) which heightens the sense of confusion conveyed by the song on page: does the song prolong the playwright's musing on his own work in the stage direction? On the stage the lines are in fact usually spoken by the First Musician, but the uncertainty of his or her identity remains throughout the song, enhanced by the shifts in time (from past to future and back again), scale (from the particular to the universal), and numerous instances of ambiguity. The phrase "I saw," particularly resonant because it is already a repetition, inscribes from the outset a theatrical dimension—a *theatron*, etymologically, is the place where one sees, from the Greek *thea*: to see.

The anonymous speaker (the playwright?) thus first speaks as a spectator, a mirror-image of the real spectators in the audience. However, s/he is watching a different stage, a different play which predates the drama that will unfold on the stage: the dismemberment of Dionysus at the hands of the Titans in mythological times, as witnessed by Athena—herself a spectator who later becomes an actor and saves his "beating heart." Indeed, the anonymous speaker's gaze ("I saw") is initially replicated by that of the "staring virgin," so that the beginning of the lyric constructs a complex, three-tiered embedding of gazes and stages. The first stanza is borne aloft swiftly on the anaphoric repetition of

"And," precipitating action until its prophetic conclusion. The final lines depart from the brisk pace and clarity of the preceding ones. In its adverbial use, "but," in "but a play," is depreciative and implies an understanding of "play" in the sense of "fake," "illusion": if the death and resurrection of Dionysus signals the end of a cycle (a "Magnus Annus") and the beginning of another, then it might be thought to lose its character of catastrophic finality. However, the phrase "As though" warns us against the naturalistic understanding of theater-as-illusion and points instead towards a ritualistic conception of theater as event. The double modulation in this line ("as though […] but") is further complicated by the shift from "Dionysus" to "God," a signifier which suggests that the death of Christ somehow replays the earlier Passion of Dionysus.

This surreptitious doubling of language is pursued in the second stanza, which ends with the apparent reprise "that fierce virgin and her Star":

> Another Troy must rise and set,
> Another lineage feed the crow,
> Another Argo's painted prow
> Drive to a flashier bauble yet.
> The Roman Empire stood appalled:
> It dropped the reins of peace and war
> When that fierce virgin and her Star
> Out of the fabulous darkness called (*CW2* 482).

The deictic "that" ostentatiously returns to the "staring" virgin of the beginning, but the fact that the "virgin" is now accompanied by a capitalized "Star" signals a difference. As Richard Ellmann observes, the "fierce virgin and her Star" now point simultaneously to three referents: Athena and Dionysus; Astraea and Spica, implicitly referenced in Yeats's ironic paraphrase of Virgil's *Fourth Eclogue* in the beginning of the stanza (with the recurrence of the anaphoric "Another", prophesying a redoubling of past events in future); and Mary and Christ, signalled by the signifier "God," the capitalized "Star," and the title of the play.[6] Creating a complex embedding of gazes and stages in language, rather than on the actual stage, and allowing denotation to branch out equivocally, the first lyric variously undermines the naturalistic paradigm, and keeps us in "fabulous darkness."

The drama proper, minimalistic as it is, pursues this game of complicating an apparently simple, straightforward storyline, and does this through a systematic doubling of basic dramaturgical elements like space and conflict; there are also two deaths and resurrections, and even two different kinds of laughter. Take the treatment of space, for instance. The stage space represents a single room, the antechamber to an inner room where the Eleven (the Apostles, minus Judas) are hiding from the Christian-hunting mob after the Crucifixion of Christ. In this antechamber three followers of Christ, a Greek, a Hebrew and a Syrian, discuss the nature of Christ and prepare to give up their lives in order to protect the Eleven. Until the final moments of the play, when the resurrected Christ appears to them, most of what happens on the stage is talk, a theological debate of sorts, and there is a long critical tradition of referring to the play as a Shavian "play of ideas."[7] But this reading disregards the fact that most of what happens in the play happens offstage. Space doubles between onstage and offstage, and offstage space is itself double: there is the inner room where the Apostles are hiding, materialized by a curtain on one side of the stage, and the street outside the window where the angry mob is expected to appear at any time. While these two areas are invisible to the spectators, they are visible to the three protagonists of the play who watch them anxiously and describe what they see to each other, and to the spectators.

The dramatic tension, which Yeats noted was sustained throughout the revised version of the play,[8] is obtained thanks to *teichoscopia* (literally, "vision from the wall"), a device originally borrowed from the epic where a character, typically, watches a skirmish from the battlements of a castle and describes it, mediating between the reader and the action proper. The three protagonists of the play thus double as spectators and narrators of offstage action, supplementing sight with speech to make this action accessible to us. The Hebrew describes the anxious vigil of the Apostles to the Greek: "If you stand here you will see them. That is Peter close to the window. He has been quite motionless for a long time, his head upon his breast" (*CW2* 483). Meanwhile the Greek generally stands at the window, watching action out on the street: "It is the worshippers of Dionysus. They are under the window now [...]" (*CW2* 486). If the play invokes the Shavian play of ideas, then it does so ironically. While the debate about the nature of Christ proves entirely sterile until the entrance of Christ himself, the epicenter of dramatic tension is systematically displaced to the margins of the stage: something is really happening, but not on the stage.

Dramatic tension, as we have seen, is based on the imminent arrival of the Christian-hunting mob, which is expected to come for the Apostles any minute. The room represented on the stage is the buffer area between the Eleven and the as-yet-unseen menace which threatens to destroy them, and the three followers of Christ make it their business to stand between them and destruction. Instructing the Greek about how to facilitate the flight of the Eleven, the Hebrew makes clear the imminence and seriousness of the danger: "We can keep the mob off for some minutes, long enough for the Eleven to escape over the roofs. I shall defend the narrow stairs between this and the street until I am killed, then you can take my place" (*CW2* 482). Yet this simple pattern is complicated by the presence of another threat—another doubling—in the streets: the frenzied worshippers of Dionysus, who terrify even the mob. Reporting what he has just seen in the streets, the Greek describes a chaotic situation:

> The followers of Dionysus have been out among the fields tearing a goat to pieces and drinking its blood, and are now wandering through the streets like a pack of wolves. The mob was so terrified of their frenzy that it left them alone, or, as seemed more likely, so busy hunting Christians it had time for nothing else (*CW2* 482).

In this description of generalized confusion which borders on the farcical, the Greek casts the entranced worshippers as a bloodthirsty "pack of wolves," a description perhaps better suited to the lynch mob which may be "terrified" by the spectacle, but is presumably more concerned to carry out its Christian-hunting mission. Thanks to *teichoscopia*, the scene is filtered through the Greek's subjectivity. While he is conscious of the real danger constituted by the mob, for whom he expresses only contempt, he is clearly more struck and repulsed by the horrible spectacle of the Dionysian parade. Here and elsewhere in the play, he speaks in the tones of the Apollonian Greek appalled by the advent of Dionysian forces, seen as fundamentally "Barbarian." The subtext here is Nietzsche's *Birth of Tragedy* (1872), which offers a mythical account of the emergence of Attic tragedy as the result of the reconciliation of Apollonian and Dionysian principles.

According to Nietzsche's mythical narrative, early Greek civilization was Apollonian; Apollo, the God of dreams, sculpture and individuation, inspired beautiful forms to men in order to shield them from the pain and horror which constitute the essence of life. These forms, best expressed by the "naïve" Homer, thus create a comforting veil of illusion. Then from the East came Dionysus, the God of music and drunken ecstasy, who takes his followers beyond the illusion of self, into a communal experience of universal suffering. Attic tragedy appears when Apollonian civilization ceases to resist Dionysism, but becomes reconciled with it. Tragedy expresses the pain inherent in worldly experience and embodied in the Passion of Dionysus, but it reveals this Dionysian essence through the appearances of Apollonian forms, thus allowing art to redeem the essential pain of life. In *The Resurrection*, the Greek features as Nietzsche's Apollonian man, rational and self-possessed, appalled by the advent of Dionysian forces which he sees as Barbarian, un-Greek influences. Watching the crowd of Dionysian worshippers in disgust from the window, he comments: "All are from the foreign quarter, to judge by face and costume, and are the most ignorant and excitable class of Asiatic Greeks, the dregs of the population" (CW2 486). Nietzsche compares the "Doric state" (of Sparta) to a war camp surrounded by hostile forces:

> For the only explanation I can find for the Doric state and Doric art is that it was a permanent *military encampment* of the Apolline: only in a state of *unremitting resistance* to the Titanic-barbaric nature of the Dionysiac could such a cruel and ruthless polity, such a war-like and austere form of education, such a defiantly aloof art, *surrounded by battlements*, exist for long.[9]

In *The Resurrection*, the push of Dionysian forces against Apollonian civilization is translated into spatial dramaturgy, and the house is constructed as a dubious fortress, besieged both by the mob and the ecstatic dancers outside the window. The Greek postures as the guardian of true Greek values against "Asiatic" Dionysian impulses. Seen through his eyes, the "monstrous ceremonies" (*CW2* 486) of the Dionysian cult are explicitly described in theatrical terms, but this is a sort of theater that threatens to bring down all the barriers that mark out and separate individuals in Greek culture. Particular anxiety is elicited by the dancers' fluid performance of gender: a "group of women" turn out to be "men dressed as women" ("What a spectacle!" the Greek gasps, *CW2* 486); a singer is described as "a girl. No, not a girl; a boy from the theatre. I know him. He acts girls' parts. He is dressed as a girl, but his finger-nails are gilded and his wig is made of gilded chords. He looks like a statue out of some temple" (*CW2* 486). Pushing irresistibly against Apollonian rationality and subjectivity yet absorbed into the existing forms of Apollonian culture, whose supreme art is sculpture, Dionysian rituals are already turning into a new form of theater.

Rewriting Nietzsche, *The Resurrection* is concerned less with the mythical death and resurrection of Dionysus than with the emergence of tragedy, a brand-new art form which appears at a moment of deep cultural upheaval in the Nietzschean narrative. In the terse dramatic economy of the play, this event is collapsed with the advent of Christianity, and the death and resurrection of the pagan god doubles as the Passion of Christ. The sacrificial goat mentioned in the Greek's description of Dionysian fury, quoted above, signals the moment when ritual coalesces into the theatrical genre of tragedy. While the exact conditions of the emergence of tragedy remain unclear, the word "tragedy" is derived from the Greek τραγῳδία (*tragôidía*), which refers to the song (*ódé*) which accompanied the ritual sacrifice of a goat (*trágos*) in Dionysian rituals. In Yeats's occult understanding of history as a succession of contrary cycles, the advent of Christianity signals the destruction of the Greek civilization, as the Greek realizes after the apparition of Christ: "O Athens, Alexandria, Rome, something has come to destroy you!" (*CW2* 492). The first stanza of the closing lyric concurs:

> Odour of blood when Christ was slain
> Made all Platonic tolerance vain
> And vain all Doric discipline (CW2 492).

While we recognize the familiar Yeatsian narrative of history, the play's emphasis on the fascinating, horrible spectacle of the Dionysian worshippers just outside the window, rewriting the Nietzschean narrative, points in another direction. I contend that in revisiting the Nietzschean myth of "the birth of tragedy," the play seeks to retrieve the conditions for the birth of a radically new form of theater in the modern age—a form brought to life in the final moments of the play with Christ's silent apparition, which tears a rent in the fabric of the wordy, sterile "play of ideas." For this new brand of modernist theater, Yeats finds an analogue in early Greek tragedy, born of the encounter of Apollonian and Dionysian forces, and he expresses the radical novelty of this new form of theater in his paradoxical handling of laughter.

In two apparently similar moments in the play, first the Greek and then the Syrian look out the window, start laughing uncontrollably, and describe scenes which strike us as particularly unfunny. In the early moments of the play, the Hebrew and the Greek confront their conceptions of Christ: the Hebrew, disillusioned by Christ's arrest and execution, argues that he was entirely human, while the Greek insists his nature is entirely spiritual. Then the Greek starts laughing:

> The Hebrew: What makes you laugh?
> The Greek: Something I can see through the window. There, where I am pointing. There, at the end of the street.
> (*They stand together looking out over the heads of the audience.*)
> The Hebrew: I cannot see anything.
> The Greek: The hill.
> The Hebrew: That is Calvary.
> The Greek: And the three crosses on top of it. (*He laughs again.*)
> The Hebrew: Be quiet. You do not know what you are doing. You have gone out of your mind. You are laughing at Calvary.
> The Greek: No, no. I am laughing because they thought they were nailing the hands of a living man upon the Cross, and all the time there was nothing there but a phantom (*CW2* 484).

The Greek laughs out of a sense of intellectual superiority. His is the subjective, Apollonian laughter of individuation: a laughter that separates him from the deluded Romans and serves to reassert his knowledge as the only valid knowledge. While the second passage is dramaturgically similar, the implications of the Syrian's laughter are in fact entirely different. Contrary to the Hebrew and the Greek, the Syrian is prepared to accept the fact that Christ may have been both human and divine—to accept the possibility of the mystery of Incarnation:

The Syrian: What matter if it contradicts all human knowledge?—another Argo seeks another fleece, another Troy is sacked.
The Greek: Why are you laughing?
The Syrian: What is human knowledge?
The Greek: The knowledge that keeps the road from here to Persia free from robbers, that has built the beautiful humane cities, that has made the modern world, that stands between us and the barbarian.
The Syrian: But what if there is something it cannot explain, something more important than anything else?
The Greek: You talk as if you wanted the barbarian back.
The Syrian: What if there is always something that lies outside knowledge, outside order? What if at the moment when knowledge and order seem complete that something appears?
The Hebrew: Stop laughing.
The Syrian: What if the irrational return? What if the circle begin again?
The Hebrew: Stop! He laughed when he saw Calvary through the window, and now you laugh.
The Greek: He too has lost control of himself.
The Hebrew: Stop, I tell you. (*Drums and rattles.*)
The Syrian: But I am not laughing. It is the people out there who are laughing.
The Hebrew: No, they are shaking rattles and beating drums.
The Syrian: I thought they were laughing. How horrible! (*CW2* 490).

In the debate between the Greek and the Syrian, we recognize the terms of the Nietzschean conflict between Apollonian and Dionysian forces. The Greek champions "human knowledge" which founds Apollonian civilization and "stands between us and the Barbarian" (a defensive position which echoes Nietzsche's metaphor of the "Doric state" as an Apollonian "military encampment"), while the Syrian is open to the possibility that Dionysian irrational forces may take us beyond the limitations of human knowledge, and allow "something else" to "appear."[10] The scene is crucial, however, not because of the philosophical debate itself, but because the terms of the debate are being acted out dramaturgically. On the one hand, the besieged house beset by the crowd of frenzied worshippers is the objective correlative of the Greek's vision of modern civilization beset by "the Barbarian." On the other hand, the Syrian's laughter signals the moment when the barbarian powers of Dionysian irrationality force their way into the fortress of Apollonian "knowledge and order." Unlike the Greek's laughter in the earlier scene, the Syrian's laughter does not separate him from others, but on the contrary, unites him with the chorus of entranced worshippers in the street. His laughter is prolonged seamlessly by the "drums and rattles" of the dancers outside, abolishing the barriers between inside and outside, a human voice and manufactured instruments, an individual body and a crowd. Again we are reminded of Nietzsche's description of "the ecstasy of the Dionysiac state, in which the usual barriers and limits of existence are destroyed."[11] In allowing Dionysian irrationality into the house, the Syrian creates the conditions for the emergence of a new kind of theater—not Attic tragedy, but its modern equivalent, a new theatrical genre outlined in the Syrian's question: "What if at the moment when knowledge and order seem complete that something appears?" and realized a few moments later with the apparition of Christ. Thus, I suggest that the Syrian embodies Yeats's ideal spectator, one who is prepared to leave behind everything he thought he knew, and to embrace theater as the experience of the impossible.

By way of conclusion I want to return briefly to the image of the "staring virgin" in the opening lyric. As we have seen, the opening line constructs the speaker as a spectator ("I saw"), but immediately undermines this privileged position with the mention of the "staring virgin." On the one hand, the vacant gaze of the "staring virgin" can be understood to mirror the speaker's gaze, reflecting his inability to see properly. On the other hand, the "stare" may suggest another modality of sight, a gaze which returns the spectator's gaze with a difference, and sees differently. What this different way of seeing might be becomes clearer if we look further in the script. The "staring" gaze of the goddess is itself replicated by the "unseeing eyes" of the Dionysian dancers at the climactic moment of their trance:

> The Greek: How they roll their painted eyes as the dance grows quicker and quicker! They are under the window. Why are all suddenly motionless? Why are all those unseeing eyes turned upon this house? Is there anything strange about this house?
> The Hebrew: Somebody has come into the room (*CW2* 491).

At one level, the "unseeing eyes" of the dancers are a mocking reflection of the hollow gaze of the three protagonists, who have spent the duration of the play frantically looking beyond the antechamber, into the inner room or out on the street, and translating sight into vacuous speech. However, the "unseeing eyes" watching the house, returning the three men's gaze with a difference, also alert us to the fact that there is another way of looking—not for what one knows and expects, but for the unfamiliar, the "strange." The apparition of Christ is just such an irruption of the "strange" into the familiar "house"—a term which also denotes a theater. In the final moments of the play, action is finally relocated to the stage, and silence succeeds to endless, sterile debate. This is a moment of epiphany—in the Syrian's words, "something appears" that exceeds human knowledge and is expressed not in words, but in dance—the mere bodily presence and movement of Christ as He crosses over to the inner room. Touching Christ to confirm that He is merely "a phantom," the Greek feels his beating heart, and screams: "The heart of a phantom is beating!" (*CW2* 491) Faced with the evidence of the contradictory nature of Christ, he finally accepts to see differently and becomes in his turn a competent spectator. The play thus delivers—gives birth to—a new form of theater which it parallels with Attic tragedy. It is an epiphanic theater which reveals the truth behind the veil of appearances—the presence of the irrational, of "something" that exceeds human knowledge. It is a theater of unveiling, which demands that the spectators let go of their previous certainties and see differently, with "unseeing eyes." It is indeed no coincidence that the inaugural stage direction, so uncharacteristically written in the first person, should be literally obsessed with curtains:

> Before I had finished this play I saw that its subject-matter might make it unsuited for the public stage in England or in Ireland. I had begun it with an ordinary stage scene in the mind's eye, *curtained* walls, a window and door at back, a *curtained door* at left. I now changed the stage directions and wrote songs for *the unfolding and folding of the curtain* that it might be played in a studio or drawing-room like my dance plays, or at the Peacock Theatre before a specially chosen audience. If it is played at the Peacock Theatre the Musicians may sing the opening and closing songs, as they *pull apart or pull together the proscenium curtain*; the whole stage may be *hung with curtains* with an opening at the left [...] (*CW2* 481; my emphasis).

At one level, of course, this passage uniquely conveys the playwright's deep personal involvement with the practical details of the performance as he envisions it, as he says, "in the mind's eye," paraphrasing the opening lyric of *At the Hawk's Well*. At another level, the highly specific stage direction comments proleptically on the subject matter of the play itself: the emergence of a modernist theater of unveiling which replicates the gesture of Attic tragedy according to the Nietzschean narrative, pulling aside the veil of appearance to reveal "the eternal primal pain, the only ground of the world."[12] As Yeats points out in his 1935 note to the play, this traumatic unveiling is understood as "a violent shock" (*CW2* 726), dramatized by the Greek's scream of terror: a shock which will deeply unsettle the spectators spiritually as well as intellectually, and ask of them that they leave behind everything they thought they knew.

The end of the play is fraught with multiple ironies. After the fleeting apparition of Christ who walks silently through the stage and exits into the inner room, the Syrian once more describes what is happening there:

> He is standing in the midst of them. Some are afraid. He looks at Peter and James and John. He smiles. He has parted the clothes at his side. He shows

them his side. There is a great wound there. Thomas has put his hand into the wound. He has put his hand where the heart is (*CW2* 492).

The end thus picks up again the device of *teichoscopia*, which has been associated throughout with the more pedestrian, common form of seeing (as opposed to the epiphanic vision experienced at the moment of Christ's apparition), and the epic mode again replaces the dramatic. The Syrian's narrative paraphrases the sanctioned narrative of the Scriptures, more specifically the episode of the incredulity of Thomas as reported in chapter 20 of the Gospel of John— an episode which is completely redundant in the play insofar as it replicates the staged epiphany of the doubting Greek only a few moments earlier. As Longuenesse comments, this speech, as well as the Greek's subsequent rather obscure quotation of Heraclitus, are "somewhat explanatory and unnecessary."[13] This anticlimactic ending perhaps makes the point that true epiphanic vision "with unseeing eyes" can only be achieved fleetingly; the effort it demands, of shedding all of one's preconceptions and certainties, cannot be sustained for longer than a few moments.

The final lyric introduces yet another change of perspective, and casts Christ's fleeting apparition in the distant past:

> In pity for man's darkening thought
> He walked that room and issued thence
> In Galilean turbulence;
> The Babylonian starlight brought
> A fabulous, formless darkness in;
> Odour of blood when Christ was slain
> Made all Platonic tolerance vain
> And vain all Doric discipline (*CW2* 492).

From the vantage point of the Musicians, singing in the present moment of the performance, the advent of Christianity is a given: it happened in the past and changed the existing structure of knowledge, for better for worse. In its original version the play ended here, but Yeats added another stanza to the 1931 version:

> Everything that man esteems
> Endures a moment or a day.
> Love's pleasure drives his love away,
> The painter's brush consumes his dreams;
> The herald's cry, the soldier's tread
> Exhaust his glory and his might:
> Whatever flames upon the night
> Man's own resinous heart has fed (*CW2* 492).

The second stanza changes tack again. Written in plodding iambic tetrameters in the gnomic present of proverbial truth, it sets out to make the rather hackneyed point of the fleetingness of all human enterprise. The final couplet, however, jolts us back into attention with its vibrant image of the flaming torch sustained by the sacrificial burning of "man's own heart": another modality of apparition, of dazzling light tearing through the nightly veil of cliché and illusion.

NOTES

1   The play was first published in *The Adelphi* in 1927, and then in a revised form in *Stories of Michael Robartes and his Friends* in 1931. It was first performed in 1934 at the Abbey Theatre in a production by Lennox Robinson. It was published in W. B. Yeats, *Wheels and Butterflies* (London: MacMillan, 1934).

2   Pierre Longuenesse, *Yeats dramaturge. La voix et ses masques* (Rennes: Presses Universitaires de Rennes, 2012), 247.

3   Helen Vendler, Yeats's *Vision and the Later Plays* (Cambridge, Mass.: Harvard University Press, 1963), 170.

4   Harold Bloom, *Yeats* (New York: Oxford University Press, 1970), 337. Quoted in Charles I. Armstrong, *Reframing Yeats. Genre, Allusion and History* (London and New York: Bloomsbury, 2013), 68.

5   Armstrong, *Reframing Yeats*, 73.

6   Richard Ellmann, *The Identity of Yeats* (Oxford: Oxford University Press, 1954), 261.

7   See for instance Peter Ure, "Yeats's Christian Mystery Plays," *The Review of English Studies* 11, no. 42 (May 1960): 171–82; Terence Brown, "W. B. Yeats and Rituals of Performance," in *The Oxford Handbook of Modern Irish Theatre*, ed. Nicholas Grene and Chris Morash (Oxford: Oxford University Press, 2016), 85. However, in his article "The Intellectual on the Stage," Tom Kilroy distances himself from this critical tradition: "If this were a play by Shaw we would have been offered a triangular debate between the three figures, on the nature of progress, perhaps, or on what constitutes the exceptional individual, the kind of person who makes a significant contribution to the evolution of the species. While Yeats's play is also highly verbal, it goes beyond language to ritual." Kilroy, "The Intellectual on Stage," *Irish Pages* 7, no. 2 (2013): 97–106, 104. My essay seeks to follow in the tracks of such a reading.

8   W. B. Yeats to Olivia Shakespear (December 27, 1930, *CL Intelex* 5428: "At the moment I am putting the last touches to a play called "The Resurrection"—young men talking [to] the Apostles in the next room overwhelmed by the crucifixion Christ newly arisen passes silently through. I wrote a chaotic dialogue on this theme some years ago. But now I have dramatic tension thought out."

9   Friedrich Nietzsche, *The Birth of Tragedy and Other Writings*, eds. Raimond Geuss and Ronald Speirs, trans. Ronald Speirs (Cambridge: Cambridge University Press, 1999), 28. My emphasis.

10   For a detailed reading of Nietzschean echoes in *The Resurrection* see Otto Bohlmann, *Yeats and Nietzsche: An Exploration of Major Nietzschean Echoes in the Writings of William Butler Yeats* (London: Palgrave Macmillan, 1982), 104–06.

11   Nietzsche, *The Birth of Tragedy*, 40.

12   Nietzsche, *The Birth of Tragedy*, 26.

13   Longuenesse, *Yeats dramaturge*, 316. My translation.

"Are you that flighty?" "I am that flighty": The Cat and the Moon and Kyogen Revisited

Akiko Manabe

In a note in *The Cat and the Moon and Certain Poems* (1924), Yeats explained that *The Cat and the Moon*[1] was "intended… to be what the Japanese call a 'Kiogen,' and to come as a relaxation of attention between, let us say, 'The Hawk's Well' and 'The Dreaming of the Bones'" (*VPl* 805). It is commonly known that the latter plays were inspired by Japanese traditional Noh, which Yeats encountered via Ezra Pound, who worked from the notes and translations left behind by the American art historian Ernest Francisco Fenollosa. The influence of the *kyogen* style, which developed in conjunction with Noh during the 14th century, is less well understood. Whereas Noh plays typically deal with serious or tragic matters rooted in history, mythology, and classical literature, *kyogen* plays are generally comical or farcical, performed between individual Noh plays in order to relieve the tense atmosphere of the Noh theater and to provoke a joyful response on the part of the audience.[2] At the center of *kyogen's* ethos is laughter—though broadly speaking there are, it must be noted, two different types of laughter that tend to be evoked. One reflects the audience's experience of delight and happiness, while the other contains an element of cruelty and often occurs in response to moments when the characters mock each other.[3]

Although Yeats's note reveals that he clearly understood *kyogen's* role, his *kyogen*-inspired play had never been performed in Japanese as a *kyogen* piece until 2015, when the prestigious Kyoto-based Shigeyama Sengoro Troupe, whose founding dates back to 1600, produced it in celebration of the 150th anniversary of Yeats's birth.[4] I was among the producers for this *kyogen*-style version of *The Cat and the Moon*, which was ultimately performed a total of nine times, including at venues in Dublin, Sligo, and Waterford during the summer of 2017 to commemorate the sixtieth anniversary of the diplomatic relationship between Ireland and Japan.[5] My discussion here of Yeats's attitudes towards laughter owes much to my involvement in these performances, to my observation of the actors' practices during rehearsals, and to our ongoing exchange of ideas about the play. Among these productions, a performance on a Noh stage in a traditional Japanese house, accommodating one hundred people for the Joint Symposium of the International Yeats Society and the Yeats Society of Japan in Kyoto in 2018, gave an ideal backdrop for exploring Yeats's theatrical philosophy.[6] This performance would certainly have satisfied his original desire for a piece that "has no need of scenery that runs away with money nor of a theatre-building" and "that can be played in a room for so little money that forty or fifty readers of poetry can pay the price" (*CW4* 173, 163). My article reveals what Yeats's play acquired through its encounter with *kyogen*, focusing on its relation to the Japanese aesthetic concept of *karumi*, as well as on the contemporary *kyogen* actors' reflections about this play that developed out of a transnational exchange between an Irish playwright and Japanese culture. I conclude with a discussion of Toyohiko Kagawa, "the Japanese labour leader and Christian saint" referenced in Yeats's introduction, who is now mostly forgotten in Japan but who exercised a crucial role in Yeats's characterization of the Saint in *The Cat and the Moon* (*VPl* 806, 808).[7]

Yeats said about this light-toned play that "no audience could discover its dark, mythical secrets" (*VPl* 806). To find these "dark mythical secrets," I will focus on an adjective, which is used six times in the play to describe the Lame Beggar and which seems to have little to do with hidden occult knowledge— the word "flighty." For scholars such as Katherine Worth, "flighty" can be defined within the basic contexts of the play as "telling lies that are bound to be found out," or it can be defined in reference to a central Yeatsian antinomy— spiritualism versus materialism (the choice in the play to be "blessed" or to be physically "cured")—whereby "flighty" means "putting a higher value on something remote and visionary… than on the material satisfaction of being able to walk."[8] This interpretation is justified, but the term takes on additional, more complicated associations when we focus on the comical words and behaviors of the Lame Beggar. It is this "flightiness" that beguilingly hides the "dark mythical secrets" from the audience, except for the selected cultured audience, or "readers of poetry," who understand Yeats's embedded philosophy. This is exactly what Yeats learned from *kyogen*, where life's deeper mysteries and complexities are given form in a casual, "flighty" depiction of a world where people readily accept whatever life offers. *Kyogen*, with laughter at its center, encompasses the daily obstacles facing individual human beings. Studying one *kyogen* piece in Fenollosa's manuscript, *Kikazu Zato*, which attracted Yeats's attention, can clarify how "dark mythical secrets" are represented in *kyogen*. Similarly, a comparison between *Kikazu Zato* and *The Cat and the Moon* will reveal how the term "flighty" is crucial to understanding both *kyogen* pieces.

Kikazu Zato belongs to a category of *kyogen* plays known as *Zato Mono* (*Zato* meaning "blind person" and *Mono* meaning "category"), in which physically disabled characters play the main roles. *Zato* originally referred to blind monks who usually played musical instruments, notably *biwa* lutes, and also sometimes chanted stories or historical legends. Yoko Sato has attempted to research the exact version of the play to which Fenollosa referred since there have been a variety of renditions depending on the *kyogen* school and the time of production.[9] As the major principle that runs through *kyogen* is common throughout the different schools, in my discussion of *Kikazu Zato* I will include another version which has been handed down and is at present used by the Shigeyama Sengoro Troupe. It explicates the earlier version called *Torahiro Bon* (Torahiro Version) of the Okura School, transcribed by Yaemon Torahiro in 1792.[10] My aim is to explain how this particular *kyogen* piece, which reveals the dark side of human beings, contains "flighty" elements as a crucial theatrical principle. In *Kikazu Zato*, a blind man, Kikuichi, and a deaf person, Taro-kaja, are ordered to look after a house while their master is away. Alone in the house together, they employ abusive language and engage in cruel behavior, as they mock each other's physical disability—which might help to explain why the play is rarely staged in Japan these days. In this particular *kyogen*, however, audience members laugh because of the characters' absurdity and playfulness, even though they are aware of the cruelty manifested in their laughter. In fact, this gets to the very crux of the matter: *Kyogen* is a drama of laughter. There is no other alternative but to laugh. Thus, by accepting reality, in this case physical disability, one accepts this as a necessary part of life.

In *Kikazu Zato*, kyogen *kouta* songs and *komai* dances reflect the psychological state of the characters and this *kyogen's* thematic motif. *Kouta* and *komai* represent *kyogen's* artistic and dramatic uniqueness, supported by an actor's mastery of stylized forms called *kata*. In this play, there are two occasions when a *kyogen* actor dances *komai* to his own *kouta* singing.[11] The first is "*Itaikeshi-taru-mono*" (pretty loveable things) in the Shigeyama Sengoro Troupe version, or "*Kazaguruma*" (a pinwheel) in the *Torahiro Bon*—these are the same *kouta* and *komai* with different titles—or "*Uji no Sarashi*" (cloth design based on the scenery of waves and a bird on the Uji River), as performed by the Izumi School. The second one is "*Tsuchiguruma*" (a cart, which is used to carry earth) in the Shigeyama and Izumi versions, or "*Itten Shikai no Nami*" (waves of the world)" in the *Torahiro Bon*. These are also the same *kouta* and *komai*, whose script and music are from the Noh play *Tsuchiguruma*, starting with "*Itten Shikai no Nami*," (pilgrims to Kumano Shrine)."[12] Actors dance and sing playfully in a "flighty" fashion. In the course of this dance, seemingly crude actions are tactically inserted. For example, Taro-kaja strokes Kikuichi's face with his foot, and Kikuichi, being blind, does not notice that it is Tarokaja's foot rather than his hand touching his cheeks. However, because the way they dance and sing is comical, graceful, and "flighty," the whole atmosphere is more jovial than callous. Without any instruments, actors sing and dance light-heartedly with delightfully rhythmical steps.

In addition, the lyrics in *utai* songs are thematically related to the context of the play. "*Itaikeshi-taru-mono*" or "*Kazaguruma*," which presents a list of children's toys and pets, fits well with Taro-kaja and Kikuichi frolicking like children. In the end, they wrestle in a manner recalling small boys at play, as Kikuichi grabs Tarokaja's legs and throws him to the ground. Yet there is no sense of violence implied here. "*Tsuchiguruma*" or "*Itten Shikai no Umi*" has a clear association with physical disability, as in the past a *tsuchiguruma* was used to carry physically disabled people. In "*Uji no Sarashi*," which was a popular song sung among people when this *kyogen* was created, rhythmical onomatopoeia such as "chiri chiri ya chiri chiri" and "karari korori" give a sense of joy to the whole atmosphere. In this way, *kyogen*'s sometimes absurd but refined way of employing dance and song is an integral part of a play.

Just as the *komai* and *kouta* contribute to the whole theatrical atmosphere in *Kikazu Zato*, the three-stanza poem "The Cat and the Moon," which is sung at three distinct places in *The Cat and the Moon*, functions as an essential thematic part of the play. In Shigeyama's *kyogen* version, the poem is sung in the *kyogen kouta* recitation style. The first stanza, sung by the Saint, impressively opens the play, mesmerizing the audience and immediately drawing them into the world of *The Cat and the Moon*. Just as this idiosyncratic image and singing style at the beginning of the play works perfectly, the third stanza which ends the play works equally well. This final stanza, both sung and danced, presents how the Lame Man and the Saint, who recently got acquainted, have now become true friends, united together as one. This process is articulated brilliantly in the *kyogen* version. First, the Saint teaches the Lame Man how to dance and sing. The Saint sings, and immediately afterward the Lame Man follows with the same words and melody. The movement of the Lame Man is, at first, very clumsy. However, gradually his dance becomes smoother and more refined. The "flighty" Lame Man's movements become lighter and more skillful. Their movements merge, and the Lame Man's movements become much more graceful. Finally, they become almost one inseparable entity. The whole atmosphere is delicately warm and soft. At first the Saint teaches him the proper way to dance, but in the end, the Saint—who originally danced in a "courtly fashion"—learns "a new dance turn" from the Lame Man, who, like a cat slowly creeping around on the ground, seems deeply rooted in the Irish soil. The Saint, on the other hand, lives in the world beyond this one. Since "two close kindred" from the two different dimensions "meet" and dance, this dance embodies the integrated state of the united Saint and Lame Man. Since the Lame Man is flighty, he can transcend the boundary between this world and the other world easily. The final dance that brings about the ultimate union reflects Yeats' understanding of *komai* and *kouta*. The whole atmosphere around these three songs and dances is in itself quite "flighty."

Andrew Parkin explains that "in Irish speech, the meaning [of flighty] is close to the 'wild' or 'full of imagination' found in Johnson's dictionary as a secondary meaning and to the 'disorderly' and 'skittish' recorded in the *OED*."[13] In the word *flighty* one hears "flight" and "light," as well as the sound "f." The image of the "light" "flight" in the air surrounds the "flighty" blessed Lame man while the "light" from outside and inside "enlightens" him. In addition, the "f" sound strengthens all these characteristics with light, dry, soft, and airy sound connotations. "Flighty" gives the Lame Man "light"-hearted and "skittish" characteristics without deep consideration, which leads to "enlightenment."

The physical movements which represent the Lame Beggar's inner state culminate in the final dance of the Lame Man uniting himself with the Saint. With reference to this final dance, Yeats explains:

> Minnaloushe and the Moon were perhaps… an exposition of man's relation to what I called the Antithetical Tincture, and when the Saint mounts upon the back of the Lame Beggar he personifies a certain great spiritual event which may take place when Primary Tincture, as I have called it, supersedes Antithetical (*VPl* 805).

The Lame Man could be the cat, Minnaloushe, while the Saint is symbolized by the Moon. The Lame Man, just like the cat, aspires to grasp something sacred in the sky and has chosen to be blessed spiritually without being cured physically. With his newly acquired blessed legs, he dances, though physically he is not cured. Still he is not used to being blessed, as his choice was made flightily and thus without deep reflection. Meanwhile the Saint, who was tired of "the courtly fashion" of this same celestial dance in his own world and was "lonely" in his sacred heavenly world, mounts the Lame Man's back and learns "a new dance turn" together with him.

Here I focus on the expression in the first stanza of the poem that represents the movement of the moon—it always "spun like a top." This suggests that on one level the Saint, who has learned the new dance step, continues to dance but never stays in the same state. On another level, this idiosyncratic description— odd because the moon in the real sky does not "spin like a top" but gradually moves in a circular orbit—catches the attention of the audience and the reader, with the top reflecting Yeats's "cones" in a "gyre" turning and never stopping. Then in the second stanza, this moon learns a new dance step from the cat. The choice of vocabulary to describe this dance step, "a new dance turn," suggests that their movements should recall Yeats's famous line, "[t]urning and turning in the widening gyre" (*CW1* 189), and that the time they are united should last only momentarily before they move on forever. This was tactfully presented in the *kyogen*-style performance held in Kyoto in 2018: the serenely exquisite *kyogen* dance of the Lame Man and the Saint, which reached the ultimate state of two beings united into one at the moment when they together look upwards—towards the moon. After this union, the Lame Man leans on his walking stick, limping--not gracefully as when he danced with the Saint a moment ago—along the *hashigakari*, which is the bridge that connects the main stage and the backstage, exiting into the backstage. Director Masumoto's interpretation suggests there will be no final state of stasis, as the gyres must always be turning. The Lame Man's spiritual legs have been blessed/cured, but not his physical legs.

In addition, the moon spinning like a top suggests a fantasy image, like those one finds in children's nursery rhymes. At the beginning of the play, this song establishes the atmosphere of the magical and mythical world of a fairy tale. The tone is flightily light, just like the tone of *kyogen kouta*. We may well remember the playfully rhythmical tone of the description of children's toys in "*Itaikeshi-taru-mono*" or "*Kazaguruma*." A *kazaguruma*, meaning pinwheel, turns endlessly through the air, similar to a top spinning. "The Cat and the Moon" is, indeed, a *kouta* song in Yeats's *kyogen*.

Since Yeats attached so much significance to this final dance, it took him fourteen years to get it right. He wanted a more energetic ending when he saw the premiere performance in 1926, so he elaborated upon it during rehearsals for a week-long run at the Abbey Theatre in 1931. Yeats realized the importance of the final dance in Noh and *kyogen*, in which the "one image" Pound and Yeats saw in both Noh and *kyogen* ultimately culminates. As Pound, drawing on Fenollosa's papers, explains:

> When a text seems to "go off into nothing" at the end, the reader must remember "that the vagueness or paleness of words is made good by the emotion of the final dance," for the Noh has its unity in emotion. It has also what we may call Unity of Image. At least, the better plays are all built into the intensification of a single Image.[14]

When the Saint tells the blessed Lame Man to bless the road, the Lame Man says he does not know the words:

> *First Musician* [i.e., The Saint]. But you must bless the road.
> *Lame Beggar.* I haven't the right words.
> *First Musician.* What do you want the words for? Bow to what is before you, bow to what is behind you, bow to what is to the left of you, bow to what is to the right of you. [*The Lame Beggar begins to bow.*]
> *First Musician.* That's no good.
> *Lame Beggar.* No good, Holy Man?
> *First Musician.* No good at all. You must dance.
> *Lame Beggar.* But how can I dance? Ain't I a lame man?
> *First Musician.* Aren't you blessed?
> *Lame Beggar.* Maybe so.
> *First Musician.* Aren't you a miracle?
> *Lame Beggar.* I am, Holy Man.
> *First Musician.* Then dance, and that'll be a miracle (*CW2* 453).

For the blessed person to give a blessing, anything that shows physicality, even words, should be unnecessary. Thus, here indeed "the vagueness or paleness of words" is superseded by the "emotion of the final dance," which is the act of blessing. In the ordinary world, a physical body dances, but the blessed one's dance should evoke and express the spiritual transcending the physical, that is, "a miracle." For in the Noh tradition, "the words," according to Pound,

> are only one part of this art. The words are fused with the music and with the ceremonial dancing. One must read or "examine" these texts "as if one were listening to music." One must build out of their indefiniteness a definite image. The plays are at their best, I think, an image; that is to say, their unity lies in the image... so also the Japanese plays rely upon a certain knowledge of past story or legend.[15]

It is worth noting here that in the *kyogen* production of *The Cat and the Moon*, the Saint was put on stage, though Yeats let the First Musician on stage speak and sing for the Saint. Yeats wanted the audience's imagination to work to the fullest, without being disturbed by the visibility of the unnecessary physical reality of the celestial Man, so he employed only voice—coming from nowhere. In contrast Matsumoto, the Japanese *kyogen* actor and director, thought the physicality or visibility of the First Musician, from whom the actual voice originates, would be an obstacle to the audience's imagination since the actor's presence before the audience is too forceful. Worth argues that "the absence of realism makes it easier to believe."[16] She is right, but in this case, rather than the absence of realism, the presence of the human body of the First Musician makes it harder for the audience to believe. Ironically, the presence of "realism," of having the actual Saint on stage, better accords with Yeats's overall desire to awaken the audience's imagination so that they might visualize all that cannot be perceived with their eyes alone.[17] Yeats's version, with no visual image of the Saint on stage, works on our imagination mysteriously, but in the *kyogen* version the physicality of the Saint is overwhelming—arrayed in his gorgeous costume and the smiling black mask which usually portrays *Daikoku*, the god of happiness and prosperity. The audience's imagination is stimulated all the more to create a specific image of this magical and mythical being with strongly human characteristics—just like the physical presence of Paula Meehan's Superman-like Saint on the dune at Dollymount Strand, Dublin in her 1995 production of *The Cat and the Moon* for children.

The decision of who should be seen on the stage and who should not, based on the subtle and delicate consideration of how the audience's imagination would work, is crucial in the actual staging of *kyogen*, since the traditional *kyogen* stage is usually an empty space. Beyond the actors' strong presences, there are no elaborate settings or props so that one's imagination is required, just as in Yeats's ideal plays created out of his encounter with Noh and *kyogen*—"[T]hese plays, which substitute speech and music for painted scenery" (*VPl* 805). The actors' words, spoken or sung, are combined with restricted acting using the formal *kata* style, thereby stimulating the audience's imagination while metaphorically painting a background scenery.

I now proceed to another aspect of "flightiness" that touches on an important element in Japanese culture and in Zen Buddhism. The principle that runs through "flightiness" is quite close to *karumi* or *karomi* (軽み), which literally translate as "lightness," in a positive sense without any associations with superficiality or capriciousness. *Karumi* is regarded as central in the poetics of *haiku/haikai*. Basho Matsuo, who established *haiku/haikai* as a distinguished literary form of poetry in the latter half of the seventeenth century, found *karumi* to be essential in his poetics near the end of his life. Basho elevated *haikai* from its original associations with comedy and even vulgarity to a more serious artistic state. His ideal poetics is achieved when one keeps one's sense and mind on "poetic sincerity," which is sophisticated, cultured, wise, and artistically elevated. By pursuing "poetic sincerity," one becomes enlightened—*satori*, the same term used in Zen Buddhism to describe the ultimate state of enlightenment achieved. Daisetsu Suzuki, whose writings on Zen fascinated Yeats, defines *satori* as follows:

> The essence of Zen Buddhism consists in acquiring a new viewpoint of looking at life and things generally. By this I mean that if we want to get into the inmost life of Zen, we must forgo all our ordinary habits of thinking which control our everyday life, we must try to see if there is any other way of judging things, or rather if our ordinary way is always sufficient to give us the ultimate satisfaction of our spiritual needs. If we feel dissatisfied somehow with this life, if there is something in our ordinary way of living that deprives us of freedom in its most sanctified sense, we must endeavour to find a way somewhere which gives us a sense of finality and contentment. Zen proposes to do this for us and assures us of the acquirement of a new point of view in which life assumes a fresher, deeper, and more satisfying aspect. This acquirement, however, is really and naturally the greatest mental cataclysm one can go through with in life. It is not easy task, it is a kind of fiery baptism, and one has to go through the storm, the earthquake, the over-throwing of the mountains, and the breaking in pieces of the rocks.
>
> This acquiring of a new point of view in our dealings with life and the world is popularly called by Japanese Zen students 'satori' (*wu* in Chinese). It is really another name for Enlightenment (*annuttara-samyak-sambodhi*).[18]

At the same time, Basho thinks that by immersing oneself in daily activities among the people, one can find one's own poetry or *haiku*. Basho's simple but profound principle shares something in common with what Yeats pursued—an artistically high, elitist poetics which cultured people would appreciate but that would, at the same time, remain connected with his ideal conception of a folk culture and of a people whose soul is rooted in traditions handed down over centuries: "we sought the peasant's imagination which presses beyond himself as if to the next age" (*VPl* 806). As Yeats explained in his note to *The Cat and the Moon*, this imagination is akin to what "Lady Gregory must have felt when at the sight of an old man in a wood she said to me, 'That man may have the wisdom of the ages'" (*VPl* 806). We should note that the subject matter of *kyogen* is often taken from the local folklore, transmitted orally over many years. To create *The Cat and the Moon*, Yeats used the legend of "a blessed well" "[a] couple of miles as the crow flies from my Galway house" (*VPl*806).

> The tradition is that centuries ago a blind man and a lame man dreamed that somewhere in Ireland a well would cure them and set out to find it, the lame man on the blind man's back. I wanted to give the Gaelic League, or some like body, a model for little plays, commemorations of known places and events, and wanted some light entertainment to join a couple of dance plays or *The Resurrection* and a dance play, and chose for theme the lame man, the blind man, and the well (*VPl* 807).

Yeats wanted to create "light entertainment" in the form of "a dance play," using a folk belief founded upon a local legend for "commemoration of known places"—all characteristics that *karumi* and *kyogen* attempt to convey.

As we have seen, *karumi* covers both a literal principle or style and a living principle or philosophy. Basho appreciated *karumi* as a poetic principle as well as a living principle, one that can be found throughout Japanese aesthetics, philosophy, and culture, and in the religious philosophy of Zen Buddhism, though the term *karumi* is not necessarily used in other arts.[19] As mentioned earlier, in order to describe the ideal poetical state, Basho used the word *satori*, which is the ultimate state for which Zen Buddhism strives. In this way, Basho's *karumi* is backed up with his understanding of Zen. Basho studied Zen, practiced *zazen* meditation seriously under Buccho, and employed Zen philosophy in his daily life. What is important in *karumi* is that it always retains the sense of joy—even in the face of bitter reality. One just laughs away any troubles or problems with a light heart—as we have seen, a familiar characteristic of *kyogen*. This leads us to what Yeats found in Zen. Yeats expressed his interest in Zen to various people, including, for example, a Japanese admirer named Junzo Sato who was sent by the Agriculture and Commerce Ministry of Japan to conduct research in Portland, Oregon. When the two met in 1920 during Yeats's American lecture tour, Sato famously presented the poet with a sword that his family had handed down for 500 years. On that occasion, Yeats talked of his fascination with Zen Buddhism. His enthusiasm endured; seven years later, Yeats wrote to Shotaro Oshima, "I am at present reading with excitement Zuzuki's [sic] *Essays in Zen Buddhism*."[20] In a letter to Sturge Moore, Yeats said, "This [Zen] seems to me the simplest and to liberate us from all manner of abstractions and create at once a joyous artistic life."[21] The reference to "This" here could be easily exchanged for *karumi*, which embodies this "joy," "lightness," and even "enlightenment" in Zen practice.

As a guiding creative principle, *karumi* can be achieved when what emerges out of a poet's intricate or complex self is expressed simply and naturally without any elaborate technical or decorative expression—the simple yet refined *haiku*. The material for such poems should be found in all that we encounter in our daily lives, where one can see the very essence of things. One can find sacredness in one's daily life, and the poems created from that experience can never be vulgar but will instead reach an elegantly sophisticated level of understanding. These characteristics of *karumi* have a lot in common with the ideals found in Pound's *Imagist* manifesto: concise expression, direct treatment of things, appreciation of nature, and the creation of integrated images.[22] Given that Pound found in *haiku* a significant breakthrough in Imagist poetics, and given the role he played in Yeats's poetic development, it was natural that Yeats should also learn from *haiku*.[23] Its result can be found not only in a *haiku*-like short poem with an explicitly Japanese title, "Imitated from the Japanese," published in 1938, but in his concisely restricted poetic style which urges one to accept reality as it is. This style became obvious in his work after his collaboration with Pound. This happy encounter with Japan answered Yeats's inner needs at a perfect time. Interestingly, Imagism did not take *karumi* seriously, but Yeats understood its essence as a crucial poetic element that he shared; and he perceived exactly the same thing in *kyogen*. *Karumi* exists in Yeats's thematic approach in *The Cat and the Moon*, which is reflected in theatrical details such as the play's language and choreography. For example, compared with other plays, in *The Cat and the Moon* the exchange of words is more rhythmical and shorter, and the actors on stage speak much less than in other plays, thus contributing to a light-hearted *karumi* or "flighty" backdrop that runs throughout the play.

We should again remember *kyogen* is a comedy or farce, a play of laughter, performed in between the more serious and tragic Noh. *Kyogen*, with its flighty or *karumi* character at its center, makes the audience relax. Protagonists of Noh are often the ghosts of famous people in Japanese history or from classic literary works, such as *The Tale of Genji* or *The Tale of the Heike*—warriors, their lovers, emperors and empresses who passed away with some strong recrimination or desire unfulfilled, or gods related to specific places.[24] Characters in *kyogen*, on the other hand, are mostly anonymous human beings, just like anyone in the audience, and their stories are often based on local folktales and beliefs rooted in the reality of common people. In the Japanese Medieval period, the life of commoners in a hierarchal feudal system, such as peasants and servants of samurai warriors, was not necessarily easy, but these commoners appear in *kyogen* with energetic personalities and are filled with life, always laughing easily in a manner that shows an acceptance of reality as it is. This means they lived flightily, with light-hearted joy as their guiding principle—with, that is, *karumi*.

It is worth noting here an idiosyncratic style of expression in *kyogen* called *naki-warai* a strange combination of simultaneous laughing (*warai*), and weeping (*naki*). Characters on stage laugh even when they face hardships, but owing to their inner sorrow they cannot help but cry, so they express these two opposite emotions simultaneously. Yeats, near the end of his life, reached a similar kind of positive state of resignation or acceptance by giving voice in his art to *naki-warai*, laughter born out of deep inner sorrow and an awareness of life's tragic reality. It is that state of "tragic joy" we find in "The Gyres" and "Lapis Lazuli." The three Chinese men carved on the piece of lapis lazuli stare "On all the tragic scene," and "Their eyes mid many wrinkles, their eyes, / Their ancient, glittering eyes, are gay" (*CW1* 301). Their laughter is light hearted and comes out of a sincere sense of joy, though it contains a deep understanding of tragedy and sorrow in life. Their laughter is the laughter of *karumi*, a reflection of *satori*.

In *The Cat and the Moon* there is only one character on stage whose "laughter" has the same kind of jovial characteristic described earlier, and that is the Saint. His laughter is visible only to the "flighty" Lame Beggar, after he is blessed.

> *First Musician.* In the name of the Father, the Son and the Holy Spirit I give this Blind Man sight and I make this Lame Man blessed.
>
> *Blind Beggar.* I see it all now, the blue sky and the big ash-tree and the well and the flat stone,—all as I have heard the people say—and the things the praying people put on the stone, the beads and the candles and the leaves torn out of prayer-books, and the hairpins and the buttons. It is a great sight and a blessed sight, but I don't see yourself, Holy Man—is it up in the big tree you are?
>
> *Lame Beggar.* Why, there he is in front of you and he laughing out of his wrinkled face (*CW2* 450).

This is the only place in the whole play where "laughter" is mentioned, and one cannot help but associate this laughter coming out of the wrinkled face with the old Chinese men in "Lapis Lazuli." The "blessed" Lame Beggar "sees" the Saint's "blessed sight" through his spiritual eyes, while the Blind Beggar who got his "blessed sight" back in his physical eyes can see everything except the Holy Man. Actually, the audience sees nothing on stage through their physical eyes, but using their "eye of the mind" (*CW2* 297) can apprehend the specific details the Blind Man lists, as well as this laughter on the wrinkled face with the Lame Man. This is the craft Yeats acquired from *kyogen*, whose stage is an empty space, forcing the audience's imagination to work to its fullest degree. (As noted earlier, our *kyogen* version put the laughing-faced Saint on stage, with the smiling black mask of Daikoku.)

Laughter or smiling here is both warm and embracing. The Saint seems to Matsumoto like *Ksitigarbha*, or *Jizo* in Japanese, adored and worshipped in Japan as a bodhisattva to protect children, as the popular folk belief goes. Its stone statues and images are everywhere on the streets. Indeed, this Saint in *The Cat and the Moon* is extremely tender and human. I cannot think of any other saint who says, "I am a saint and lonely" (*CW2* 449). This Saint wants to find a friend. The Lame Man, being flighty, casually thinks getting blessed may be "grand." He does not reflect on this deeply but says, "I will stay lame, Holy Man, and I will be blessed" (*CW2* 450), which sounds like "I can be your friend." In addition, after the Saint has blessed the Lame Man, even the Saint himself seems not so sure if the Lame Man appreciates what he has done for him, so he asks "Are you happy?" after he gets up on the Lame Man, sounding very human. This image resonates with the previous image of the Lame Man atop the Blind Beggar. Unlike the Blind and the Lame, two separate beings, one atop another, who were constantly fussing about their own respective problems, the Lame Man and the Saint become united, merged into one as friends. Matsumoto's image of this Saint as a *Jizo*, this adored figure in Japanese folk culture, perfectly captures what Yeats tried to convey. St. Colman, being a Christian Saint, has been worshipped reverently, but at the same time, like the holy well, he also has a deep association with Celtic local beliefs. By evoking this friendly saint of the well, Yeats tried to communicate the Irish spirit or soul, the spirit of the Gael, and the mythic world of Celts and Druids. The language used in the exchange of the Lame Man and the Blind Man is also Hiberno-English, with highly unique Irish characteristics, meant to communicate the Irish spirit or soul to the audience.

Yeats says, "Belief is the spring of all action; we assent to the conclusions of reflection but believe what myth presents; belief is love, and the concrete alone is loved" (*VPl* 806). People have accepted the "belief" about the "myth" of the well of Saint Colman whom they "love" and who loves them. And the Saint in *The Cat and the Moon* is a "concrete" being, not a "conclusion of (abstract) reflection." The two Beggars who believed the myth took "action" and came to the well. Their "spring of action" was the desire to be blessed or cured, and they had their wishes fulfilled. Belief in Irish local myth can be a source of action; indeed, Yeats hoped the Irish people would take action to fulfill their nationalistic ideal after watching the plays he and Lady Gregory put on at the Abbey Theatre.

The now-blessed Lame Man says, "Why, there he [i.e., the Saint] is in front of you and he laughing out of his wrinkled face." The Lame Man has acquired (spiritual) sight, allowing him to see the Saint, while the Blind Man is finally able to see this world but not the world beyond, the spiritual world. The Saint's laughter is not resigned or dry but instead is a warm expression of happiness. Interestingly enough, in our *kyogen* version, there was another character who gave an impressive laughter in a very different style and with a very different meaning. It was the Blind Man, who laughed in a loud voice—in a special *kyogen* style, which is essential to this form of theater—when he exited from the stage after beating the Lame Man in a stylistic movement based on *kata*, with the accompanying *kyogen* expression of "*Yattona Yattona*,"[25] though Yeats's script just says "*The Blind Beggar goes out*" (*CW2*, 452). Matsumoto's interpretation embellishes this even further. The beating could be seen as an expression of human cruelty. However, this *kyogen* production does not give the impression of too much cruelty, partly because of *kyogen*'s comically stylized movement and the tone of voice adopted by the two actors. Another reason originates in the way the story flows in this production. Because the Blind Man, being blessed, gets his sight back, naturally he becomes extremely happy. Among the things he enjoys seeing is the skin of his own black sheep on the Lame Man's back. The "flighty" Lame Man continues to tell his lie that the sheepskin is white, just as he did when the Blind Man did not have his eyesight. The exchange between the Blind Man and the Lame Man is resonant of a children's quarrel, like the exchange of the blind Kikuichi and the deaf Taro-kaja. The Blind Man, now having his eyesight back, wants to use this newly given ability, just like a child wanting to try out a new toy. The moment he can see the world, he excitedly catalogues all that he sees, as if the entire world is made up of objects, like the list of toys in "*Itaikeshi-taru-mono*," there for his delight. He thus exerts his energy outwards toward the Lame Man, whose lie triggers his beating at the hands of the Blind Man. The Blind Man is now happy to go around by himself without the Lame Man's help, so laughingly he disappears from the stage—with Sengoro Shigeyama's impressive *kyogen* laughter, filled with life's energy. In this way, essentially the Blind Man's beating and laughter are also quite "flighty."

I conclude here by introducing Toyohiko Kagawa, "[t]he Japanese labour leader and Christian saint" who, I believe, contributed to Yeats's creation of the Saint. In his letter to Oshima dated August 19, 1927, Yeats wrote that he had

> read Toyohiko Kagawa's Novel which is translated into English under the title "Before the Dawn," and find it about the most moving account of a modern saint that I have met, a Tolstoyan saint which is probably all wrong for Japan, but very exciting to an European....[26]

In his note to *The Cat and the Moon* Yeats mentions Kagawa twice:

The Japanese labour leader and Christian saint Kagawa… speaks of that early phase of every civilisation where a man must follow his father's occupation, where everything is prescribed, as buried under dream and myth. (*VPl* 806).

…to study natures that seemed upon the edge of the myth-haunted semi-somnambulism of Kagawa's first period. Perhaps now that the abstract intellect has split the mind into categories, the body into cubes, we may be about to turn back towards the unconscious, the whole, the miraculous. (*VPl* 808).

Kagawa, first of all, is here designated as a "Christian saint," related to both "myth" and "dream," which are connected to "the unconscious, the whole and miraculous"—everything Yeats cherishes. Kagawa's first period can be traced in his autobiographical novel *Before the Dawn*.[27] Kagawa went back and forth on the border between life and death, first infected with dysentery at the age of seven and then with tuberculosis at nineteen. Miraculously returning to full health, Kagawa decided to devote his life to people who were suffering in extreme poverty at the bottom layers of society and chose to live in a slum in Kobe, where he took care of the poor, the sick, and children. During his childhood he was desperately unhappy, the illegitimate son of a declining merchant family that eventually went bankrupt. His father was an enlightened politician while his mother was a *geisha*, and both of them passed away when Kagawa was only five. He was then raised by his grandmother and his father's legitimate wife, who treated him cruelly. Two American missionaries he met in his teens saved him, and he became an ardent Christian, fired with a sincere belief in God's love that drove him to work in the slums. Although he was beaten, attacked, and robbed, he was finally accepted and was able to improve the living standards of those living in poverty, especially with respect to the education of children.

The details of Kagawa's life shed light on how we might interpret the actions of the Blind Beggar and the Lame Beggar in *The Cat and the Moon*. The Blind Man's newly acquired eyesight originates in a blessed miracle, and yet these miraculous eyes are what enable him to attack the Lame Man, who has worked as his eyes for forty years. The Lame Man steals the Blind Man's black sheep, and even after being blessed, still flightily goes on lying to him about his innocence, although he is wearing the obvious evidence of his robbery. Both cases show that even after they have encountered the Saint, they go on being sinful. People in the slums beat Kagawa up like the Blind Beggar and robbed him like the Lame Man, but these actions only strengthened Kagawa's acceptance of the fallible nature of all human beings and deepened his commitment to better their lot. The fundamental attitude of the Saint in *The Cat and the Moon*, marked by warm acceptance and laughter, is also that of Kagawa, who offered acceptance despite extreme violence and lies. Kagawa is an embodiment of the

Saint in *The Cat and the Moon*, and the two main characters in the play are beggars, whose position in society is equivalent to that of the people in the slum. Kagawa, especially in "his first period," thus inspired Yeats's depiction of the Saint and, equally important, reinforced his commitment to a form of drama, exemplified by *The Cat and the Moon*, that seeks "wisdom, peace, and communion with the people" (*VPl* 806).

In the final dance, "two close kindred" from two different dimensions "meet" and dance with a newly acquired "dance turn," and the integrated state of the Saint and the Lame Beggar is momentarily revealed. Still, everything turns around eternally on the gyre like a spinning top. Therefore, at the end of the play, the Lame Beggar, just like Minnaloushe, "creeps through the grass," "lifts to the changing moon / His changing eyes," rising from this world adoring the moon, the metaphoric equivalent of the Saint.

NOTES

1   Written in 1917, the play was first published in *The Criterion* and *The Dial* in 1924, and was included in *The Cat and the Moon and Certain Poems* (Dublin: Cuala Press, 1924). It was first performed at the Abbey Theatre on May 9, 1926. The final version was published in *Wheels and Butterflies* (London: Macmillan, 1934) after the emendation done during the 1931 production at the Abbey Theatre. I am grateful to the *kyogen* actor Kaoru Matsumoto, who showed insightful understanding of the play in his direction of *The Cat and the Moon* in the Japanese *kyogen* style, and offer special thanks to Ian Shortreed for proofreading an earlier version of this paper. This paper is supported by JSPS KAKENHI Grant Number JP17k02542.

2   In addition to acting in a separate *kyogen* repertoire, *kyogen* actors also play important parts in Noh plays. Both the sections of Noh plays in which *kyogen* players act and also the *kyogen* players' role in those sections are called *ai* or *ai-kyogen*. *Ai-kyogen* characters sometimes work as narrators, explaining the whole scene, as reporters giving information to the main characters, or as comical characters doing something foolish, often becoming a key to a crucial turning point in a drama. They are integral parts of the drama, but at the same time they contribute an unusual objectivity, from quite a different perspective. You may well see similarity in the two old men appearing at the beginning of *The Player Queen* (*VPl* 715–16).

3   At present two schools of *kyogen* exist, the Izumi School and the Okura School. Most of the time each school performs independently, but sometimes actors of both schools perform on the same stage. Their dramatic principles are fundamentally the same, but slight differences do exist. The most popular and active group of the Izumi School is the Nomura Family, based in Tokyo, while that of the Okura is the Shigeyama Sengoro Family in Kyoto. The crucial difference between the two troupes lies in their treatment of laughter. The Shigeyama Sengoro Troupe regards laughter as a core element, putting the utmost emphasis on laughter in their dramaturgy (Interviews with Sengoro Shigeyama XIV and Kaoru Matsumoto; I have interviewed both *kyogen* actors frequently since 2004.) Regarding actual performing practice, I owe a lot to my direct communication with the Shigeyama Sengoro Family; thus, Yoko Sato's paper stating that Nomura Mansai ranks laughter as their troupe's third priority gave me a shocking surprise: "Nomura Mansai, a very popular *kyogen* actor who has attempted a number of global collaborations, states that his father, Nomura

Mansaku, designated as a living national treasure, always encouraged him to achieve 'beauty first, amusement second and laughter last.'" Yoko Sato, "Yeatsian Heroes and Laughter," *Journal of Irish Studies* XXXIV (Tokyo: IASIL Japan, 2019): 50. Sengoro XIV, the grandson of the late Sensaku IV Shime, who was also designated as a living national treasure and was a mentor to Matsumoto, learned that laughter is central in their craft. Akiko Manabe, "W. B. Yeats and *Kyogen*: Individualism and Communal Harmony in Japan's Classical Repertoire," *Études Anglaises: revue du monde anglophone* (octobre-decembre 2015): 425–41.

4   Performed at Kobe Gakuin University, November 10, 2015, as a part of the 370th Kobe Gakuin University Green Festival, produced by Professor Shigeru Ito. The script was translated into Japanese by Tetsuro Sano and the play was directed by Kaoru Matsumoto. The Blind Beggar was played by Masakuni Shigeyama (present Sengoro Shigeyama XIV), the Lame Beggar by Shigeru Shigeyama, and the Saint by Senzaburo Shigeyama. In Yeats's original the Saint does not appear on stage but the First Musician speaks/sings in his stead; in this production an actor portrays the Saint. I will explain the meaning of this below.

5   These productions had the same personnel as in note 4, except that the Saint was performed by Kaoru Matsumoto. The Irish performances took place at Smock Alley Theatre, Dublin (July 24, 2017); Factory Performance Space, Sligo (July 27, 2017); and Garter Lane Arts Centre, Waterford (July 29, 2017).

6   Directed by Kaoru Matsumoto at Kashokaku Noh Stage in Kyoto, December 15, 2018. The Blind Beggar was played by Sengoro Shigeyama XIV, the Lame Beggar by Shigeru Shigeyama, and the Saint by Kaoru Matsumoto.

7   Yoko Sato has recently written on *kyogen* and *The Cat and the Moon*, focusing mainly on the play's conclusion and on the symbolic importance of sound. See "Yeats's 'Kiogen': The Symbolic Structure of *The Cat and the Moon*," *Irish University Review* 47, no. 2 (2017): 298–314.

8   Katherine Worth, *The Irish Drama of Europe from Yeats to Beckett* (London: The Athlone Press, 1986), 181.

9   Yoko Sato, "Fenollosa's Manuscript of *Kikazu Zato*, The Japanese Source of Yeats's *The Cat and the Moon*," *Journal of Irish Studies* 30 (Tokyo: IASIL Japan, 2015): 27–38.

10   *Kikazu Zato*, 『不聞座頭』, transcribed and handwritten by Sensaku Shigeyama III, Masakazu. I was allowed to see this manuscript, which is privately owned by the Shigeyama Sengoro Family, by their special permission. *Okura Torahiro Bon Noh Kyogen*, ed. Takashi Sasano (Tokyo: Iwanami, 1945).

11   Traditionally, *kyogen* actors were male. Quite recently, women have practiced *kyogen*, especially at the amateur level, but still almost all professional *kyogen* actors are men. Therefore, I use gender-biased pronouns when referring to *kyogen* players.

12   For this second kouta/komai, Izumi Manzaburo Family employs "Kumano Doja" (pilgrims to Kumano Shrine). According to Sato, no other groups except the Izumi Matasaburo Family has the *komai* "Kumamo Doja." Sato, "Fenollosa's Manuscript," 34.

13   W. B. Yeats, At the Hawk's Well *and* The Cat and the Moon, *Manuscript Materials*, ed. Andrew Parkin (Ithaca, NY: Cornell University Press, 2010), 214.

14   Ernest Fenollosa and Ezra Pound, *The Noh Theatre of Japan, With Complete Texts of 15 Classic Plays* (Mineola, NY: Dover Publications, 1917, 2004), 45–46.

15   Fenollosa and Pound, *The Noh Theatre of Japan*, 63.

16   Worth, *The Irish Drama of Europe*, 181.

17   When Paula Meehan produced *The Cat and the Moon* for children at Dollymount Strand in Dublin, she let two actors mingle with the kids throughout the morning as "just a couple of vagrants on the beach." Then, suddenly, the actors began to perform *The Cat and the Moon* on the spot. Regarding the Saint, Meehan, like Matsumoto, "had an actor, who looked a bit like Superman in his face make up and body suit, rise from a big barrel which acted as the holy well." When the play ended, one of the boys who "had a beautiful Dublin voice"

sorrowfully asked the Saint to give him back his boy's voice instead of his girlish voice, for which he was bullied not only by other boys but also his father. This shows that the physicality of the Saint rendered the play genuinely and realistically close to the truth. Paula Meehan, "Paula Meehan recalls a day when a troupe of Dublin actors wished they had magic powers," *Irish Times* (August 24, 1996); https://www.irishtimes.com/news/paula-meehan-recalls-a-day-when-a-troupe-ofdublin-actors-wished-they-had-magic-powers-1.79922.

18 "D.T. Suzuki, *Essays in Zen Buddhism* (London: Souvenir Press, 2010, digital edition, 2011). Daisetsu Suzuki, *Zen* (Tokyo: Chikuma Shobo. 1987), 187.

19 Taizo Ebara points out that the spirit that respects lightness, close to Basho's *karumi*, could be found in various kinds of art such as *renga* poems, *kado* (flower arrangements), *sado* (tea ceremonies), *gagaku* (traditional Japanese music), and the visual arts. See Taizo Ebara, "*Karumi no Shingi*" (True Meaning of *Karumi*), *Basho Kenkyu* (Basho Study) No. 2, (1943), referred to by Hana Kaneko, "A History of 'Karumi' Researches: from The Taisho Era to 30s of The Showa Era," *Bulletin of the Graduate School, Toyo University* 50 (2014), 18. My discussion of *karumi* here owes an enormous debt to Kaneko's three-part article, "A History of 'Karumi' Researches," in *Bulletin of the Graduate School, Toyo University* 50 (2014): 13–35; 51 (2014): 49–65; and 52 (2015): 85–99.

20 Shotaro Oshima, *W. B. Yeats and Japan* (Tokyo: Hokuseido Press, 1965), 125–27, 6. Sean Golden kindly let me read two sets of his masterworks on Zen and Yeats, prior to their publication. One includes his contributions to the collection *Yeats and Asia*: "Introduction," "The Ghost of Fenollosa in the Wings of the Abbey Theatre," and "Yeats on Asia." See *Yeats and Asia: Overviews and Case Studies*, ed. Sean Golden (Cork: Cork University Press, 2020). The other is his article, "W. B. Yeats and Laughter: Wit and Humour, Irony and Satire, Zen and Joy," *Yeats Studies, the Bulletin of the Yeats Society of Japan* no. 50 (2019); 3–27. They are among the best studies published on Yeats and Zen. I do not refer to details of his studies in this paper but I would like to acknowledge their significance here.

21 *W. B. Yeats and T. Sturge Moore: Their Correspondence 1901–1939* (London: Routledge & Kegan Paul, 1953), 69, cited by Hiro Ishibashi, *Yeats and the Noh: Types of Japanese Beauty and their Reflection in Yeats's Plays*, ed. Anthony Kerrigan, no. VI of the Dolmen Press Yeats Centenary Papers MCMLXV (Dublin: Dolmen Press, 1966), 194.

22 Ezra Pound, *Literary Essays of Ezra Pound*, ed. T. S. Eliot (New York: New Directions, 1918, 1968), 3.

23 Indeed, there were other Japanese individuals who introduced *haiku* and Noh to Yeats, notably Yone Noguchi, but it is Pound whose contribution inscribed these Japanese elements into Yeats's poetics most forcefully.

24 Pound and Yeats were drawn to the highly sophisticated form of Noh called *Fukusihi Mugen Noh*—whose literal translation is a double-layered dream-fantasy Noh play. *Fukushiki Mugen Noh* is divided into two scenes. In the first half, a ghost of the protagonist appears as a living human being, while in the second half the same protagonist dramatically shows his or her real identity as a ghost.

25 This expression—exclamation and onomatopoeia—is used when actors engage in an action requiring some strength or power. Depending on the situation, the movement may require huge effort but sometimes just a small amount of power. Actors use this expression sometimes slowly, sometimes quickly. For example, they may say "*Yattona Yattona*" when they carry a log up or down a hill; when they sit down or stand up; when they latch or unlatch a door; when, acting as thieves, they creep through a hole made in a hedge. This versatile expression can be used in various situations, and there is not one specific meaning.

26 Oshima, *W. B. Yeats and Japan*, 6–7.

27 Toyohiko Kagawa, *Shisen wo Koete* (*Beyond the Border between Life and Death*) (Tokyo: Kaizo Sha, 1920). Its English version is *Before the Dawn*, trans. by J. Fukumoto and T. Satchell (New

York: George H. Doran Company on Murray Hill, 1924). Other major references to Kagawa are *Comic: Shisen wo Koete* (Tokyo: Ie no Hikari Kyokai, 2009), Mikio Sumitani, *Kagawa Toyohiko* (Tokyo: Iwanami, 2011), Tadashi Mikyu, *Kagawa Toyohiko Den* (Tokyo: Bungeisha, 2020), and the home page of the Kagawa Archives & Resource Center, accessed January 10, 2020; https://t-kagawa.or.jp/. I would like to express my gratitude to Michael McAteer for reminding me of Kagawa.

A Review of *Science, Technology, and Irish Modernism*

Kathryn Conrad, Cóilín Parsons, and Julie McCormick Weng, eds., *Science, Technology, and Irish Modernism* (Syracuse: Syracuse University Press, 2019), paperback, pp. 405, ISBN 978-0-8156-3598-7.

Reviewed by Lloyd (Meadhbh) Houston

One of the most fruitful areas of the "expansion" which has characterized the "New Modernist Studies" has been the growing attention that has been paid to the role of science and technology as concepts, discourses, and transformative socio-political forces in nineteenth and twentieth-century culture.[1] In the last two decades, an array of studies have emerged which answer Mark S. Morrison's call for critics to embrace a fundamentally interdisciplinary model of "scientific and technical modernism" which attends to what Gillian Beer has identified as the "two-way" traffic of "ideas," "metaphors," "myths," and "narrative patterns" between scientists and non-scientists which marked the period.[2] However, with a few notable exceptions, scholars have been slow (if not actively reluctant) to extend this analytical framework to Ireland and its culture.[3] Under such circumstances, the fifteen essays that comprise *Science, Technology, and Irish Modernism* constitute not only a timely intervention in Irish Studies, but also a robust contribution to the history and philosophy of science in Ireland.

As Kathryn Conrad, Cóilín Parsons, and Julie McCormick Weng point out in the introduction to their path-breaking collection, received critical wisdom has tended to exceptionalize Irish cultural attitudes to science and technology, which have traditionally been presented as uniformly hostile. However, as the diverse array of material surveyed in the collection makes clear, while many Irish cultural figures regarded the "scientific worldview" as an unwelcome colonial imposition, this did not preclude them from dramatizing its impact in their works, or from trying to envisage alternative modes of scientific endeavor and technological innovation. Indeed, some of the collection's most rewarding essays attend in detail to the idiosyncrasies of Ireland's efforts to cultivate (or synthesize) an autochthonous brand of scientific, technical, and cultural modernity, such as the establishment in 1940 of the Dublin Institute for Advanced Studies (DAIS), a pet project of Éamon de Valera, which brought together the Schools of Theoretical Physics and Celtic Studies, and provided an academic home to Erwin Schrödinger following his flight from Nazi-occupied continental Europe. For Andrew Kalaidjian, the DAIS provides a crucial context for reading texts such as the late Flann O'Brien (Brian O'Nolan) novel, *The Dalkey Archive* (1964), in which the protagonist envisages a collaborative encounter between James Joyce and the mad scientist, De Selby, the outcome of which would be a book sufficiently "recondite, involuted and incomprehensible" to "be no menace to universal sanity."[4] Luke Gibbons, in an essay whose diffuse but evocative form replicates the montage effects with which it is concerned, offers a reading of the Easter Rising as a surreally "Modern Event," peopled by Chaplain impersonators, matinée idols, and posters for an array of "cancelled futures" (63)—performances that would not take place, to be held in theaters the Rising would destroy, in a nation that had been changed utterly. In a high-point of the collection, Susanne S. Cammack explores how Lenox Robinson—playwright, manager, producer, and director at the Abbey Theatre from 1909 till his death in 1951—deploys a malfunctioning gramophone in his 1925 drama *Portrait* as a metaphor both for the traumatized psychological state of the play's male protagonist and for the as yet unreleased political tensions of an Ireland tentatively emerging from over a decade of sectarian violence, anti-colonial struggle, and civil war: "an Irish gramophone, enacting an Irish cultural anxiety" (136).

Surveying a broad stretch of Irish cultural history, from the nascent revivalism of the 1880s through the "high" modernism of the 1920s, to the "late" modernism of the 1930s and, in some instances, far beyond, the collection is admirable in its scope and in its attention to both major and minor figures in the Irish modernist canon. Thus, while Synge, Joyce, Beckett, and Bowen make expected appearances, so do less often canvassed figures such as Emily Lawless and Seumas O'Sullivan. Likewise, while prose fiction and drama comprise the lion's share of the material under consideration, admirable attention is paid to formats that feature less prominently in traditional accounts of Irish modernism, such as Joyce's vinyl recordings or Denis Johnson's BBC and RTÉ radio plays, and the complex negotiations of cultural capital which attended their engagement with these signally modern forms. Damien Keane's essay on Joyce's recording of an excerpt from the "Aeolus" episode of *Ulysses* (1922) not only provides a detailed account of the fractious negotiations between the Society of Authors (Joyce's estate), the Poetry Collection at the University of Buffalo (which held copies of the rare recording), Folkways (a record label associated with spoken-word performance), and Caedmon (a record label associated with prestige recordings of authors) which dogged efforts to reissue the reading in the 1960s, but also reflects valuably on the ways in which "the reproduction of a gramophone recording" became the stage for "the reproduction of social relations" between a range of artistic, scholarly, and commercial institutions as a result (155). Likewise, Jeremy Lakoff's essay on Johnson explores how the young playwright, himself a radio and television producer at the BBC, developed a "hypermediated" mode of metadrama that deployed decidedly modernist aesthetic strategies to unapologetically "middlebrow" ends (162, 170). Alongside its attention to these technological developments, the collection offers a wide-ranging account of Irish modernism's engagement with a range of scientific theories and disciplines, including natural history, eugenics, psychoanalysis, and the "new physics." In a tour-de-force of close reading and nuanced historicism, Enda Duffy traces Joyce's pointedly medicalized attention to his characters' pulses, impulses, and other physiological indices of "aliveness" through the pages of *Ulysses*, linking this "new protocol of modernist representation" to the vibrant research culture of nineteenth-century Irish medicine, the expansion of the nation's public health infrastructure in the aftermath of the Famine, and long-standing characterizations of the Irish as preternaturally nervous and predisposed to mental illness (187). While Duffy's assertion that, through Joyce's fiction, "the protocols of the Irish nineteenth-century medicoclinical gaze become the literary modus of modern Irish fiction" may be something of an overstatement (201), he makes a compelling case for analyzing Irish modernism in light of the social history of medicine.

In the course of the collection's fifteen essays, it is the revival and late modernism which are the most decisively reconsidered. Challenging traditional constructions of the revival as uncomplicatedly anti-scientific and anti-modern in orientation, Seán Hewitt explores the ways in which revivalists adopted decidedly modern scientific techniques to critique the abstraction and alienation to which they felt scientific and technical modernity could give rise. Building on the work of Sinéad Garrigan, Mattar and others, Hewitt explores the ways in which Lawless, Synge, and O'Sullivan—all of whom were keen naturalists— deployed the discourses and methodology of natural history to "re-enchant" the natural world and imbue the primitive with a spiritual dimension which the positivism and secularism of Enlightenment reason had threatened to efface (29).[5] As Hewitt's close-reading of their fiction and non-fiction writing reveals, for these figures, the mysterious spiritual charge of the natural environment did not reside "beyond" but "within" its material forms (21), and was best apprehended through the scientific modes of close observation practiced in the naturalist field clubs to which all three authors belonged. In a similar vein, Alan Graham reveals the extent to which degenerationist and eugenic models of physical and cultural decline were central to both the theory and rhetoric of revivalism in Ireland. As Graham rightly emphasizes, while critics may wish to quarantine the presence of eugenic thought in twentieth-century Irish culture to what they present as a belated flirtation on the part of an aging Yeats, in reality, its influence was widespread among cultural nationalists of every stripe, particularly where issues of language revival and the English popular press were concerned. Indeed, if there is a limitation to Graham's persuasive and well-evidenced essay, it is only that it does not pursue the influence of eugenic thought further into other areas of the cultural life of twentieth-century Ireland, such as the debates surrounding the 1929 Censorship of Publications Act and its proscriptions on printed material pertaining to birth control and abortion, to which a broad spectrum of Irish modernists vigorously contributed.[6] Rounding out the collection's reconsideration of the revival are essays by Weng and Conrad, who explore the relationship between revivalists and technology. On the one hand, Weng offers an intriguing portrait of John Eglinton (William Fitzpatrick Magee) as an "Irish Futurist" who "viewed machines as vehicles that could advance cosmopolitan impulses in Ireland and Irish literature" by serving as "ambassadors" between individuals, communities, and nations (35, 36, 45). On the other hand, Conrad explores the more ambiguous and ambivalent attitude to technology manifested in Tom Greer's proto-modernist dynamite novel, *A Modern Daedalus* (1885), in which, Conrad argues, cutting-edge weapons technology comes to function as an avant-garde "medium of expression" in an emergent mass-media culture (82). In both cases, Joyce figures as a key inheritor and interpreter of these (admittedly idiosyncratic) modes of technologically inflected revivalism, extending, rather than repudiating their pointedly Irish approach to technology. For Weng, though Eglinton theorized an aesthetic of cosmopolitan materialism, it was Joyce who would most fully and concretely manifest its possibilities through stories like "The Dead" (1914), in which gaslight and electric light eventually allow Gabriel Conroy to experience a new sense of connection to his wife Gretta, her deceased sweetheart, Michael Furey, and their shared homeland, in all its heterogeneity. For Conrad, the influence of Greer's novel and its protagonist hover in the background of Joyce's work, informing both the character of Stephen Dedalus and his ambivalent attitude to the modern technological networks (or "nets") which Eglinton had so celebrated: "Instead of escaping," Conrad argues, "Joyce suggests the artist's need to fly *by means of* those nets" and, in so doing, acknowledges their capacity both to liberate and constrain (94).

If the contributions of Hewitt, Graham, Weng, and Conrad are valuable because they challenge long-standing critical truisms concerning the revival, the essays which deal with late modernism in Ireland are valuable because they constitute robust contributions to a critical discussion still in its infancy. For Kalaidjian, traditional theorizations of late modernism, which focus on British responses to the uncertainty generated by the Second World War and the unravelling of the Empire, do not fit the Irish case, because Irish neutrality in the "Emergency" arguably meant that the Irish state had never been more drearily secure.[7] In Kalaidjian's account, the work of late Irish modernists such as Brian O'Nolan (Flann O'Brien, Myles na gCopaleen, et al.) is characterized by an investment in uncertainty which grew in direct proportion to the mundane certainties of life in the mid-century state. According to Kalaidjian, the late Irish modernist "turns to uncertainty not," as in the case of their high modernist predecessors, "because Ireland itself is murky," but because "Ireland—as a nation—is entirely too real" (248). For Parsons, projects such as John Banville's 'science tetralogy"—a loose series comprising *Doctor Copernicus* (1976), *Kepler* (1981), *The Newton Letter* (1982), and *Mefisto* (1986)—embody a form of late modernism that simultaneously "trades in and rejects the very temporality of lateness," deploying "astronomical" scales of time to question "received ideas of the time of modernism" (266, 265, 266). Belatedness and anachronism also surface in Chris Ackerley's essay on "Samuel Beckett and the Biological," which explores the author's consistent preference for outmoded theorizations of the organic world derived largely from Wilhelm Windelband's *History of Philosophy* (1893)—a key source for the soon-to-be-published "philosophy notes"—and Ernst Haeckel's *The Riddle of the Universe* (1899), whose account of "larval consciousness" Ackerley posits as a key inspiration for his 1953 novel, *The Unnameable* (226). In different ways, all three essays offer a vivid sense of what Irish Studies and Science Studies can offer Modernist Studies in its approach to late modernism, while, at the same time, providing a valuable starting-point for future efforts to conceptualize "lateness" in a specifically Irish context.

As the editors readily admit, Yeats, who famously dismissed "the man of science" as one who had "exchanged his soul for a formula," might seem to cut an unusual figure in such a collection.[8] Yet, while Yeats is often held responsible for the popular image of the revival as fundamentally anti-materialist and anti-scientific in bent, as Ronan McDonald and others have shown, his professed animosity towards contemporary scientific thought often occludes the oblique yet significant ways in which it shaped and inflected his writing.[9] A recent special issue of the present journal on "Yeats and Mass Communications" edited by David Dwan and Emilie Morin paints a very similar picture regarding Yeats's relationship to technology. Though he preferred to "cast himself as a dilettante, a dissenter, or a naïve observer" of the proliferation of "mass media" and its attendant technologies, as Dwan and Morin note, Yeats regularly exploited them with the proficiency of "a master."[10] *Science, Technology, and Irish Modernism* valuably extends this more nuanced consideration of Yeats's response to scientific and technical modernity by exploring the ways in which it informed his work for theater, in theory and practice. At the more abstract end of the spectrum, Gregory Castle offers a Deleuzoguattarian reading of Yeats's Cuchulain plays as "machinic assemblages" which increasingly eschew a model of cultural authenticity rooted in "painstaking fidelity" to "well-ordered archives" that "attest to a truthful [...] version of past events" in favour of the "creative potential" that arises from the "intransmissibility" of those events and their "aura" (101, 99, 98):

> When Yeats reimagined the story of Cuchulain, the Iron-Age hero of the Red Branch of Ulster, he sought a new pathway through technological modernity: his dramatic productions superadded to the legend the basic mechanics of modern theatre as well as avant-garde innovations that sought to undermine them. He worked with translations by [Standish] O'Grady and [Augusta] Gregory, but in large measure fashioned his own machinic arrange of the story, an arrangement that accommodated tradition as something *added to* the work[.] (102–03).[11]

Another area of machinic arrangement to which Castle draws attention is Yeats's dramaturgy, particularly his engagement with the aesthetic practices and stage techniques of Japanese Noh theater in plays such as *At the Hawks Well* (1917), which Castle argues provided the formal "basis for the break with traditions that he contemplate[d] in his aristocratic 'inventions'" and had "the machinic effect of eliminating the temporal and geographical distance between the audience and the legendary story" (104, 105). While Castle gestures towards the "material limits of theatre" and their impact on Yeats's "machinic" drama, his commentary largely remains confined to the level of textual analysis (96). A more historicist account of the ways in which the stage machinery of the Abbey Theatre served to realize (or constrain) Yeats's vision in these plays might have served to concretize Castle's claims. This is suggested not to criticize Castle's piece, which offers a nuanced account of the decidedly modern ways in which figures such as Yeats, O'Grady, and Gregory approached questions of tradition and authenticity, than to highlight its status as something of an outlier in a volume which otherwise approaches the topic of "technology" in more literal terms.

More materialist in approach (if not in subject matter) is Katherine Ebury's essay on "Science, the Occult, and Irish Drama," which charts the ways in which the "new physics" informed Yeats and Beckett's staging of occult phenomena and ghostly apparitions. Surveying the plethora of popular science publications which sought to communicate Einstein's work on relativity to a mass audience, Ebury illustrates how "ghostly metaphors were written into the new physics and how it was received" from the outset, particularly where light was concerned (235). On the one hand, as Michael Whitworth has argued, the finite velocity of light—a central constant in Einstein's mathematics—and, by extension, the notion that the past is preserved in travelling light rays, conferred a "patina of modernity" to the literary tropology of the restless dead.[12] On the other hand, as Ebury notes, quantum theory's image of light simultaneously behaving as a wave and a particle destabilized its status as a reliable constant, conferring upon it, in aesthetic terms, both "realistic" and "surrealistic" properties (231). For Yeats, who read Einstein's *The Meaning of Relativity* (1922), Bertrand Russell's *ABC of Relativity* (1925), Alfred North

Whitehead's *Science and the Modern World* (1925), and Arthur Eddington's *The Domain of Physical Science* (1925), among others, the new physics appeared to bear out his convictions concerning the "limitations of nineteenth-century positivist science" (235). More than this, it offered a scientific sanction for occult research into the "unseen" and "unknown," which, Ebury argues, manifested itself in the "increasing prominence" of "ghostly light" in plays such as 1936's *The Words Upon the Window Pane* and 1938's *Purgatory* (239). However, as Ebury shows, though Dublin theaters experimented with "black light" (ultraviolet) techniques in the 1920s and 1930s, the Abbey's lighting rig remained decidedly conservative, changing little from its installation in 1904 until the theater's destruction by fire in 1951. As such, Ebury argues, it was not until productions such as James Flannery's contentious "expressionistic" rendering of *Purgatory* at the 1990 Yeats Theatre Festival that the full dramaturgical implications of the playwright's interest in the "difficult light of the new physics" and its occult ramifications were thoroughly explored (243). An unintended boon of such productions, Ebury argues, is the way in which they illuminate the hitherto under-acknowledged debt which Beckett's later "haunted" dramas owe to Yeats's "occult theatre" (243). In Ebury's view, plays such as *Footfalls* (1976) manifest not only a decidedly Yeatsian desire to "make it ghostly"—a direction Beckett gave to Billie Whitelaw in its inaugural production—but an interest in the occult potential of modern lighting techniques derived from the "new physics" which had inspired the older writer.[13] In Ebury's compelling reading, "Yeats's interest in the science of light demonstrates that he is less antiscientific than is typically perceived, while Beckett's interest in the occult reveals that he is more Yeatsian than is expected" (230). In its examination of the mechanisms of cultural exchange between literature and science in the early twentieth century, its close attention to the relationship between technology and aesthetic form, and its desire to put pressure on received narratives of modernism and modernity in Ireland, Ebury's essay exemplifies the virtues of a collection that will be indispensable to scholars and students of Irish modernism, the cultural revival, and the history of science in Ireland alike.

NOTES

1   Douglas Mao and Rebecca L. Walkowitz, "The New Modernist Studies," *PMLA* 123, no. 3 (May 2008): 737.
2   Mark S. Morrisson, *Modernism, Science, and Technology* (London: Bloomsbury Academic, 2017), 7. This call to action was first issued in Mark S. Morrisson, "Why Modernist Studies and Science Studies Need Each Other," *Modernism/Modernity* 9, no. 4 (2002): 675–82. Representative examples of this critical turn include Tim Armstrong, *Modernism, Technology, and the Body: A*

Cultural Study (Cambridge: Cambridge University Press, 1998); Michael H. Whitworth, *Einstein's Wake: Relativity, Metaphor, and Modernist Literature* (Oxford: Oxford University Press, 2001); Heike Bauer, *English Literary Sexology: Translations of Inversion, 1860–1930* (Basingstoke: Palgrave Macmillan, 2009); Katherine Ebury, *Modernism and Cosmology: Absurd Lights* (Basingstoke: Palgrave Macmillan, 2014); Paul Peppis, *Sciences of Modernism: Ethnography, Sexology, and Psychology* (Cambridge: Cambridge University Press, 2014).

3   Recent exceptions include Gregory Castle, *Modernism and the Celtic Revival* (Cambridge: Cambridge University Press, 2001); Sinéad Garrigan-Mattar, *Primitivism, Science, and the Irish Revival* (Oxford: Oxford University Press, 2004); Rónán McDonald, "'Accidental Variations': Darwinian Traces in Yeats's Poetry," in *Science and Modern Poetry: New Approaches*, ed. John Holmes (Liverpool: Liverpool University Press, 2012), 152–67; Rónán McDonald, "The 'Fascination of What I Loathed': Science and Self in W. B. Yeats's *Autobiographies*," in *Modernism and Autobiography*, ed. Maria DiBattista and Emily O. Wittman (Cambridge: Cambridge University Press, 2014), 18–30; Emily C. Bloom, *The Wireless Past: Anglo-Irish Writers and the BBC, 1931–1968* (Oxford: Oxford University Press, 2016).

4   Flann O'Brien, *The Complete Novels* (New York: Alfred A. Knopf, 2007), 712.

5   James F. Knapp, "Primitivism and Empire: John Synge and Paul Gauguin," *Comparative Literature* 41, no. 1 (1989): 53; Garrigan-Mattar, *Primitivism, Science, and the Irish Revival*; Giulia Bruna, *J. M. Synge and Travel Writing of the Irish Revival* (Syracuse, NY: Syracuse University Press, 2017).

6   Seán Kennedy, "First Love: Abortion and Infanticide in Beckett and Yeats," *Samuel Beckett Today/Aujourd''hui* 22 (2010): 79–91; Lloyd (Meadhbh) Houston, "'sterilization of the Mind and Apotheosis of the Litter': Beckett, Censorship, and Fertility," *The Review of English Studies* 69, no. 290 (January 31, 2018): 546–64; Seán Kennedy, "Beckett, Censorship and the Problem of Parody," *Estudios Irlandeses* 14, no. 2 (October 31, 2019): 104–14; Lloyd (Meadhbh) Houston, "Beckett in the Dock: Censorship, Biopolitics, and the Sinclair Trial," *Estudios Irlandeses* 14, no. 2 (October 31, 2019): 21–27.

7   Kalaidjian has in mind studies such as Tyrus Miller, *Late Modernism: Politics, Fiction, and the Arts Between the World Wars* (Berkeley: University of California Press, 1999) and Joshua Esty, *A Shrinking Island: Modernism and National Culture in England* (Princeton, NJ: Princeton University Press, 2004).

8   W. B. Yeats, "'Poetry and Science in Folklore," in *Uncollected Prose*, ed. John P. Frayne, vol. 1 (London: Macmillan, 1970), 174.

9   Garrigan-Mattar, *Primitivism, Science, and the Irish Revival*, chaps. 2–3; McDonald, "Accidental Variations"; McDonald, "The 'Fascination of What I Loathed': Science and Self in W. B. Yeats's *Autobiographies*."

10   David Dwan and Emilie Morin, "Introduction: Yeats and Mass Communications," *International Yeats Studies* 3, no. 1 (November 2018): 1.

11   Emphasis in original.

12   Whitworth, *Einstein's Wake*, 178.

13   Quoted in Mary Luckhurst, "Giving Up the Ghost: The Actor's Body as Haunted House," in *Theatre and Ghosts*, ed. Mary Luckhurst and Emilie Morin (Houndsmills: Palgrave Macmillan, 2014), 163.

A Review of *A Reader's Guide to Yeats's A Vision*

Neil Mann, *A Reader's Guide to Yeats's A Vision* (Clemson, SC: Clemson University Press, 2019), pp.408, ISBN: 978-1-942954-62-0, $130.

Reviewed by Claire Nally

Anyone familiar with Yeats's intimidating but rewarding occult work, *A Vision*, will be well-acquainted with Neil Mann's comprehensive website, www.yeats-vision.com, as well as his authoritative and lifelong academic work focusing on that topic. As such, the publication of his book, *A Reader's Guide to Yeats's A Vision* will be met with some delight by Yeats scholars everywhere. Mann's latest publication aims to render *A Vision* more accessible to academics, students, and, I think, general readers interested in this mysterious text. The book also anticipates some prior knowledge of the topic, insofar as "it is written foremost for those who have already examined *A Vision* and want to understand it better" (vii). Despite this, the author is clearly mindful to make Yeats's occultism more intelligible, given the fact that each chapter in *A Reader's Guide* is organized as two parts: a shorter, summary section ("Overview") which outlines the key issues and a longer section ("In Further Detail") which offers scholarly context and more extensive treatment of important references.

As Yeats was a veteran editor and re-editor of his work, it will come as no surprise that whilst Mann pays more attention to the second published edition of *A Vision* (1937), he also maintains a clear engagement with the 1925 version, and notes that his *Guide* can be used to elucidate either version. As such, Mann's comprehensive navigation of the wealth of manuscript material relating to *A Vision* and its authorship is also extremely valuable here. The *Reader's Guide* draws clear correlations between the biographies of Yeats and Georgie Hyde-Lees, the assembly of the manuscripts that became the multi-volume *Vision Papers*, and a reading of the published version(s), as well as an introduction to the actual process of writing the material that became *A Vision* (automatic writing, the "sleeps," and the intervention of the mysterious Instructors and Frustrators). At the same time as Mann devotes a high level of detail to elucidating these concepts, he also expands upon the contexts through which we can read *A Vision*, one of which is philosophy. Mann explains that Yeats certainly thought of his work in a philosophical tradition, but one which we might think of as pre-Cartesian, insofar as it relates to metaphysical philosophy and writers such as Plato, the Neo-Platonists, and even the pre-Socratics. Noting that "what is possible and inventive in one age is outmoded and archaic in another," Mann stylishly notes that thereby "Yeats's system takes on the appearance of 'rejected knowledge,' one of the definitions of the occult" (44). If we think of *A Vision* in this way, its status as an occult text is somewhat up for debate. The fact that it is often not considered a "legitimate" work of philosophy as much as one of eccentricity and arcane lore is very much subject to its anachronism in the twentieth century. In aligning *A Vision* with pre-Enlightenment philosophy, Mann suggests that *A Vision* represents a somewhat more persuasive system for understanding the world.

Mann's book is divided into sections, rather than following the chronology of either the 1925 or 1937 versions. As such, the reader who would like to focus on specific areas or themes, such as the *Daimon* or the Four *Faculties*, can easily identify a relevant chapter. A thematic arrangement such as this also means that a whole section is devoted to key areas, such as "Gyres and Geometry." Wrestling with perhaps one of Yeats's more familiar occult symbols, Mann sympathetically offers a reading of those twin cones from a philosophical perspective, stating that "Yeats's conception of cosmos is idealist" (53), but he also at this point unpacks the theory of the gyres with several interpretative illustrations. Of especial note here is how Mann identifies the significant aspects of this theory (helpfully arranged as bullet points (56–57), which certainly helps to contextualize the wider ideas related to the phases of the moon, the cycles of history and time, and the role of the Thirteenth Cone. Similarly, the chapter entitled "History: Cycles and Influx" expands upon the exposition of history which is the hallmark of so many anthologized and popular Yeats poems, including "Leda and the Swan," "The Second Coming," and a host of other examples. As Mann explains, "[these poems] make more sense when readers appreciate how Yeats saw the ebb and flow of the tides in human history" (267). Mann situates *A Vision* here as articulating the oscillation of religious dispensations and those of civilization (269), and offers this reading through the lens of Yeats's familiar symbolism. For instance, in discussing the two annunciations of *A Vision*, and that anticipated in a future cycle, Mann explains that "Such a change is imminent and, in the poem 'The Second Coming,' Yeats asks what kind of annunciation there might be" (269). As such, Mann's discussion is also extremely useful for both undergraduate and postgraduate students seeking in-depth background knowledge of the poems but wanting to do so from the perspective of Yeats's more arcane thinking. However, lest a reader think that the accessible nature of the *Reader's Guide* necessitates a simplistic approach to Yeats, it is worth noting that the allusions to philosophy, classic sources, and literary reference points are extensive. In one short discussion of the Great Year, Mann outlines the influence of Ptolemy, Hipparchus, and Spenser's *The Faerie Queene* alongside a lucid discussion of how the Great Year functioned for the ancients. Vico, Hegel, and Spengler are all carefully recognized as part of Yeats's research, but again, these complexities do not overshadow the major objective, which is to unpack *A Vision* for the reader.

Mann's scholarship also outlines the editorial and textual emendations which characterize the differences between the two versions of *A Vision*, and the text spends some time addressing how Yeats's style can be both poetic and obtuse, scientific, and explanatory. Related to this idea of style and accessibility, Mann situates *Per Amica Silentae Lunae* (1917) as a useful prelude to the complexities of *A Vision*: "What were suggestive juxtapositions in *Per Amica Silenta Lunae*, where the reader has to supply something to reach understanding, become frustrating *non sequiturs* in *A Vision*, where the reader is simply perplexed" (60). It is this comprehensive engagement with Yeats's other works which establishes not only *A Vision's* importance to the symbolism of the poetry and plays, but its integral role in understanding Yeats's thought.

For those scholars wishing to follow up on Mann's sources, a bibliography would have been useful, in addition to the extensive explanatory notes at the end of the text. However, it would be churlish to regard this publication as anything other than foundational in terms of introducing *A Vision* to a new generation of readers, as well as supporting current scholarship as a reference aid. It is also a thoughtful corrective to those who have dismissed *A Vision* as simply Yeats's "silliness" or his "Southern Californian" intersts, as W. H. Auden famously claimed. Rather, this is a realistic but non-judgmental examination of the limitations, complexities, and rewards involved in studying *A Vision*. Mann expands upon this in "Reframing *A Vision*," noting that whilst readers may have been frustrated by Yeats's lack of clarity about his theory, at the same time, the importance of this work cannot be underestimated, "whether a key to Yeats's poetic symbolism or an astrological key to life" (295).

As a note of caution, whilst Mann suggests that "*A Vision* puts forward no clear morality, but the concepts that emerge from its understanding of human life and history are profoundly humanist, pluralist and tolerant" (297), it is very much the case that *A Vision* cannot be depoliticized or dislocated from some of Yeats's other works (*On the Boiler* being a notable example, as well as his infamous marching songs). So, I do wonder if there is a rather optimistic reading in Mann's claim that "outside of the framework of reincarnation, the shift is one of empathy: that many approaches to a good life are very different, and that there, but for the grace of God, go you or I" (297). Yeats's assertion of the rights and freedoms of individuals was applicable only to certain people at specific times; his earlier socialism gave way to a much more disenchanted politics, and I cannot help but wonder if this is being glossed over here.

In final praise of the volume, it is also very much the case that whilst this Guide identifies a number of key scholars in this very specific field of Yeats studies (Kathleen Raine, Colin McDowell, Warwick Gould, Margaret Mills

Harper, and of course, George Mills Harper), the critical and theoretical positions of these writers do not intrude upon Mann's objective to explain *A Vision*, and he does not merely put forward another argument which contributes to the already expansive body of *A Vision* criticism. Essentially, this book is not about uncovering a submerged reading of *A Vision*, but rather, it is a stylish teaching tool, a research aid, and a companion to Yeats's occult philosophy.

A REVIEW OF *THE COLLECTED LETTERS OF W. B. YEATS VOLUME V: 1908–1910*

John Kelly and Ronald Schuchard, eds. *The Collected Letters of W. B. Yeats Volume V: 1908–1910* (Oxford: Oxford University Press, 2018), cxi + 1179 pp., ISBN 978-0-19-812688-1.

Reviewed by Maria Rita Drumond Viana

On January 12, 1909 Yeats wrote to John Quinn, who was then receiving his own (multiple) copies of the long-awaited *Collected Works* in eight volumes and declared that "one never really understands one's own writings till they have been beautifully printed" (*CL5* 394). This collected edition of 1908, printed by A. H. Bullen at the Shakespeare Head Press, can be seen as one of the biggest personal achievements of the very busy three-year period covered in *The Collected Letters of W. B. Yeats Volume V*, edited by John Kelly and Ron Schuchard—the latest installment in another long-going collected works project, this time with Oxford University Press (OUP). I can only imagine that these modern editors, and Kelly in particular as the general editor for the whole project, must feel the same way whenever a new volume comes out. As a reader and a scholar especially interested in letters I am evidently attached to the materiality of paper and ink, but in the case of Yeats's correspondence it could be argued that, with the *InteLex Past Masters English Letters* database of all the extant letters, the content of the letters themselves is reasonably well-known to subscribers and thus the frisson caused by each newly published volume would be lessened.

This assumption is wrong on at least two counts: firstly, it takes for granted that every university library can afford to subscribe to *InteLex* and other such databases—something that may be true for many European and North American universities but is definitely not the case in developing countries such as my own (Brazil). As individual subscriptions are often too expensive or simply unavailable, the promise of widespread online access remains just a promise. Secondly, and more in tune with Yeats's own realization as reported to Quinn, there are connections that can only be seen when beautifully printed. As with the 1908 *Collected Works*, this beauty refers to a lot more than just the quality of the paper, binding, and type, and includes organization (the ordering of parts being a particularly salient point in the Yeats-Bullen negotiations) and, very importantly, standardization—the effect of which is a sense of visual unity, so dear to Yeats. These have been qualities of the *Collected Letters* project from the start, and the passage of time seems to have made the editors ever more sensitive to it.

Of course, some of the editorial practices adopted are part of OUP's (as well as other major academic presses') mandates for similar projects. Nevertheless, a simple comparison with the *Letters of William and Dorothy Wordsworth*, edited by Alan G. Hill (also for OUP) and finished around the same time the Yeats project started, reveals a big difference in editorial practices: the sheer amount of paratext (understood here as anything-but-the-letters) that Kelly and the other editors make available in each volume is unrivalled, and has in fact reached an all-time high in this fifth installment. While most of the elements have been present since Volume I, including the chronologies (expanded for each period considered—and also published in a separate volume that reads almost like an appointment diary of Yeats's activities, meetings, travels, writings, and even dreams), the volume introductions serve as biographical essays that, if collected and printed, could rival Roy Foster's magisterial two-volume biography—in size, if not in scope. Though always anchored in the letters, with specific reference to relevant pages, these introductions do more than contextualize them or make thematic and chronological sense of this mass of materials—no mean feat in itself.

I have chosen to highlight the impressive scholarly achievement of volume V in particular—the bulkiest in the series thus far despite covering only a period of three years—in an attempt to account for the thirteen-year gap since volume IV appeared. I confess, I shared the impatience of many, even if some of the texts included here can be found and are annotated not only in *L* but also in *UP*. That these texts appear in the latter volume as stand-alone prose pieces highlights the characteristic of the letter as / not a genre—to borrow from the brilliant article by Margaretta Jolly and Liz Stanley. Kelly's expansive definition of what constitutes a letter is notable and considers the communicative and reciprocal aspects of the epistolary act. In addition to various materials in the form of enclosures (such as draft proposals), it has been the editors' practice to include "ghost-letters" that, though lost or untraced, are made present in the book from "references in replies, memoirs, diaries, and so on" (*CL5* xlvi). More interestingly, for me, is the decision to "reproduce printed dedications to books when *cast in epistolary form*" (*CL5* xlvi, emphasis added). Though the specifics of the form are not made explicit, from the examples found throughout the collection I gather that it includes the usual triad of addressee(s), some more or less definite dating, and the signature(s), indicating audience, occasion and author respectively. The editors also recognize changes in function, stating that "[o]n occasion, his letters were sub-edited into the form of articles, and we have included any item for which there is internal or external evidence that this has occurred" (*CL5* xlvi). This is true for some of the pieces that appear in *UP1* and *UP2*, sometimes with no mention of their epistolary origin.

Yet this can also be true of the aforementioned dedications, an example of which is a letter of dedication of volumes one and two of *Plays for an Irish Theatre* to Lady Gregory, which appeared in the May 1903 edition of *Where There is Nothing* and was subsequently included in *VPl* (232). This is one of the more public recognitions of Gregory's creative role in the writing of *Cathleen ni Houlihan*—"*We* turned my dream into the little play" (*CL3* 322, emphasis added)—an example of a public letter which, despite being open and visible to others, reinforces the bond between sender and addressee, and can be understood within Marcel Mauss's "the system of the gift."

More than ever, and particularly after the cerebral hemorrhage she suffered on February 2, 1909, Lady Gregory appears as someone who truly had "been more to me than father or mother or friend, a second self. The only person in the world to whom I could tell every thought" (*CL5* 413). A quick glance at the excellent resource that is the list of recipients (presented in alphabetical order of addressee with page numbers and, more helpfully, separate from the general index—a care not always taken in many letter collections) clearly reveals Augusta Gregory as the main node of Yeats's correspondence network—despite the fact that he still spent a considerable amount of time in Coole and would not, during these periods, be required to write to his friend.

Of course, we mostly get Yeats's side of it— "mostly" because the copious notes (in the *belles notes* tradition) very often reproduce excerpts from letters to Yeats, particularly when they're alluded to in the main letters. In Yeats's case we are, fortunately, blessed with a veritable cornucopia of printed sources and my survey of the various interests and editorial principles reveals both differences in market appeal and changes in academic practices, coupled with questions of etiquette and the complicated copyright status of the missives themselves. If the practice of a family returning the letters kept by a deceased member to their original senders has faded alongside the popularity of letter-writing itself, it was never an uncomplicated matter, as the recently revealed correspondence between T. S. Eliot and Emily Hale has made painfully clear.

A culture of celebrity, sometimes more than mere interest in history-writing, also explains why some letters by famous figures are kept—and published. In Yeats's case, two friends, to whom he wrote extensively in different periods of his life, published from his letters when he was still alive and in the same year, to very different effects. The first was Katharine Tynan, whose *Twenty-Five Years: Reminiscences* (1913) included unauthorized transcriptions of their correspondence and was met with ire; the second was Lady Gregory herself, whose *Our Irish Theatre* (1913) alluded to the many missives exchanged, and whose later *Hugh Lane's Life and Achievement, with some Account of the Dublin Galleries* (1921) included direct transcriptions of letters from Yeats, who widely supported both ventures.

It is more common, however, to find letters published after the person's death, sometimes hot on its heels, as is the case of Dorothy Wellesley's *Letters on Poetry from W. B. Yeats to Dorothy Wellesley*, written in 1939 and published in 1940. Despite the misleading name, this is in fact an example of crossed correspondence, since it contains letters from both writers, as well as notes and reflections by Wellesley herself. A contemporary volume of crossed correspondence that is as thorough as the *CL* but whose purpose is closer to Wellesley is Ann Saddlemyer's *W. B. Yeats and George Yeats: The Letters* (*YGYL*). Showing all sides of the conversation (in fact not limited to W. B. and George), it also shows a relationship based on many common interests, and not just poetry.

The third kind of edited volume is the passive correspondence, best represented by Richard Finneran, George Mills Harper, and William M. Murphy's two-volume *Letters to W. B. Yeats* (1977). *The Gonne-Yeats Letters*, edited by Anna MacBride White and A. Norman Jeffares (*G-YL*), could also be included under this category of passive correspondence in spite of the title, which effectively suggests a crossed-correspondence. The choice is justified by the presence not only of many fewer messages from the Yeats side of the conversation (30 against 372), but also because those are from a much later period and do not exactly configure a dialogue with the other letters present.

I can only imagine how many more volumes of passive correspondence the editors of the *CL* would have filled had they been given the opportunity to edit the materials they evidently have consulted for the notes. The expansiveness of volume V certainly suggests that they see their remit as being much more than simple organizers of materials, and while the inclusion of J. M. Synge's last will and testament may seem a bit much, I cannot deny it is a wonderful resource to have in the appendix. But how soon can I get hold of volume VI?

NOTES

1.   Alan G. Hill, ed., *Letters of William and Dorothy Wordsworth*, 8 vols. (Oxford: Clarendon Press, 1967–1993).
2.   Margaretta Jolly and Liz Stanley, "Letters as / not a genre," *LifeWriting* 1, no. 2 (2005): 1–18.
3.   See Alan T. McKenzie, *Sent as Gift: Eight Correspondences from the Eighteenth Century* (Athens, GA: University of Georgia Press, 1993), 3.
4.   Marcel Mauss, *The Gift: Forms and Functions of Exchange in Archaic Societies* (London: Routledge, 1954).
5.   Maria Cramer, "The Love Letters of T. S. Eliot: New Clues into his Most Mysterious Relationship," *New York Times*, Jan. 4, 2020.
6.   Katharine Tynan, *Twenty-Five Years: Reminiscences* (New York: Devin-Adair, 1913); Lady Augusta Persse Gregory, *Our Irish Theatre* (New York and London: G. P. Putnam's Sons,

Knickerbocker Press, 1913; Lady Gregory, *Hugh Lane's Life and Achievement, with Some Account of the Dublin Galleries* (London: William Clowes and Sons, 1921).

7. Dorothy Wellesley, ed., *Letters on Poetry from W. B. Yeats to Dorothy Wellesley* (London: Oxford University Press, 1940).

8. Richard Finneran, George Mills Harper, and William M. Murphy, eds., *Letters to W. B. Yeats*, 2 vols. (London: Macmillan, 1977).

Precarious Bodies and Physical Theater: A Review of DancePlayers' *The Dreaming of the Bones* by W. B. Yeats

The Dreaming of the Bones, by W. B. Yeats, performed by DancePlayers Company, O'Donoghue Theatre, Galway, Ireland, November 7–10, 2019.

Reviewed by Zsuzsanna Balázs

Dance and physical theater companies have been on the rise in Ireland over the last few years, including BrokenTalkers, the Blue Raincoat Theatre Company, Pan Pan Theatre, CoisCéim Dance Theatre, the Liz Roche Company, and most recently, DancePlayers Company. DancePlayers was founded in 2018 by Galway-based director and researcher Melinda Szűts with the aim of reimagining Yeats's dance plays through physical theater and demonstrating the ability of Yeats's plays to reach contemporary audiences. Initially, this rising popularity of physical theater was more visible at the fringes, but lately it has moved towards the center, as Helen Meany has explained in her article "Physical theatre comes to town." After their acclaimed debut with *The Only Jealousy of Emer* at the Galway Theatre Festival in 2018, DancePlayers returned with an equally powerful performance of Yeats's 1919 Noh-theater inspired dance play *The Dreaming of the Bones* in November 2019.

Both plays include ghosts and supernatural elements, and thus feature precarious, liminal bodies whose visibility depends on the decisions and choices of other characters—bodies that try to but cannot act as agents of their own fate. In Irish theater and society, the Irish Body has always been a political arena through which questions of the nation and sexuality have been contested and interrogated. As Claudia Kinahan put it in her article "Irish Bodies: The Rise of Dance Theatre," the Irish body has often occupied a liminal and vulnerable position, and it has always been a site of conflict in the national imagination, which became more visible at events such as the recent fight for abortion rights or the decriminalization of homosexuality in 1993. Yeats's plays frequently deal with the complex relationship between the nationalist master-narrative and sexual desire, although the bourgeois nationalist audiences of Yeats's time, viewed this as an insulting and dangerous combination. His plays thus often confront the audience with difficult questions, such as "is sexual desire a figuration of politics, or politics a displacement of sexual desire?" As Nicholas Grene has observed with regard to the riots after the opening of John Millington Synge's *The Playboy of the Western World*: "As the repressed physicality of the sexual was allowed to appear from under the normal decencies of its covering, so sex was proximate to violence [...]. Such contamination of confused categories was a deeply disturbing affront to the middle-class nationalist community whose self-image depended on just such moral classification."

Yeats was also aware that *The Dreaming of the Bones* might cause some turmoil; hence its premiere was delayed until 1931. On June 6, 1918, he wrote to Ezra Pound that he saw it as a "doubtful" play and that "recent events in Ireland have made it actual & I could say in a note that but for these events I should not have published it until after the war. I think it is the best play I have written for some years" (CL *InteLex* 3447). It is also less frequently emphasized that Yeats engaged critically with contemporary debates about both normative and non-normative forms of desire. He often expressed his sympathy for those who differed from the norm in any way (including Edward Martyn, Oscar Wilde, Charles Ricketts, Lawrence of Arabia, and Roger Casement among many others), and who could not fulfil their desires because of some obstacle created by society or the state. In a letter to Lady Dorothy Wellesley on December 2, 1936, Yeats criticizes those political and social institutions which shame people because of their difference. Here Yeats clearly states that saving a nation cannot serve as an excuse for such public shaming:

> But suppose the evidence had been true, suppose Casement had been a homo-sexual & left a diary recording it all, what would you think of a Government who used that diary to prevent a movement for the reprieve of a prisoner condemned to death? Charles Ricketts & Lawrence of Arabia were reputed homo-sexual [*sic*] suppose they had been condemned on a capital charge some where [*sic*], what would you think of a proffession [*sic*] who insured their execution by telling the middle classes that they were homosexual. [...] I can only repeat words spoken to me by the old head of the Fenians years ago. "There are things a man must not do even to save a nation" (CL *InteLex* 6737).

The *Dreaming of the Bones* dramatizes the clash between the nationalist master-narrative and sexual desire in the context of Ireland's colonial past. As Kinahan explains, dance and physical theater can offer "theatre makers a universal language through which to reinterpret difficult stories about our past and the contested political status of our bodies." In the past, Irish politics and the Catholic Church made several efforts "to enforce their ideology by de-sexualizing and repressing the Irish Body." In the play, the ghosts of Diarmuid/the Stranger (played by Jérémie Cry-Cooke) and Dervorgilla/the Young Girl (Kashi Cepeda) ask forgiveness for the sin they committed against the Irish nation—that is, falling in love with each other resulting in the Norman invasion and pushing the Irish nation into slavery. More broadly speaking, the play is about the precariousness and liminality of two Irish people who cannot fulfil their love for one another and who ask for visibility, recognition, and forgiveness from another Irishman, the Young Man (John Rice): "If some one of their race forgave at last / Lip would be pressed on lip" (*VPl* 773). The Young Man is fleeing from the police after the Easter Rising, and here he seems to represent the nationalist master-narrative of duty and sacrificial politics: adhering to a conservative code of value both in term of theater and politics, he wants to exclude sexual desire from the national cause. Thus, the play interrogates whether the Young Man is justified in shaming and excluding two Irish people from the frameworks of recognition as a way of taking revenge for the country's colonial past.

Using physical theater helps to challenge and resist such conservative nationalist paradigms of sexuality and puts the marginalized in center position. It also highlights those areas that homogenizing political discourses want to hide from the public eye, namely the merging of the national and the sexual. The Young Man in this play refuses to merge the two realms and condemns those who have done so, but Yeats seems to offer a more critical take on his character. The play raises more sympathy for the lovers but it also helps understand the Young Man's standpoint, which became even more evident through the choreography in DancePlayers' production. As the performance made clear, the play does not want audiences to take sides necessarily, but allows both the Young Man and the ghosts to tell their stories through interwoven and visually clashing narratives.

In this review I explore how the precarity of Diarmuid and Dervorgilla was framed by the production's dramaturgical devices (movement, music, costume, and masks) and how these devices helped associate their vulnerable position with the fragility of birds, thus raising more sympathy for the lovers. I reflect also on two more questions central to the play and the production: What is it exactly that the Young Man is rejecting, and what is the play interrogating with this representation of the legend?

Before the show began, the First Musician (Conor Gormley) was already center stage as the audience arrived and took their seats. His body was in the center but in a precarious pose: its crouched, exposed position suggesting a state of physical precarity, such as subjugation and vulnerability, as if he was praying or begging. This image already conveyed important messages about power and the vulnerability of the body, putting the arriving audience in a somewhat superior position.

Along with Gormley's first movements the music began, composed specifically for this production by Hungarian composer Ákos Lustyik and performed by Gergely Kuklis (violin), Nicola Geddes (cello), and Gilles Dupouy (harp). The slow, codified movements and white body paint of the three musicians also evoked Butoh performance techniques—a Japanese physical theater which merges Western and Eastern theatrical conventions in a similar manner to the influence of Noh theater on Yeats's plays. The Second and Third Musicians

Figure 1. The First Musician (Conor Gormley) before the beginning of the performance. Photo credit: Emilia Lloret

(Aimee Banks and Una Valaine) joined him in this opening sequence, and their bent, crouching poses and terrified facial expressions put them in a dramaturgically inferior position, foreshadowing the fate of the ghosts of Diarmuid and Dervorgilla. The first lines of the opening song already indicate the importance of excess, desire, and emotions in this play: "Why does my heart beat so?" (*VPl* 762); "They overflow the hills, / So passionate is a shade, / Like wine that fills to the top / A grey-green cup of jade" (*VPl* 763).

Jérémie Cry-Cooke created a spectacular choreography of precarity through an interesting representation of agency and its precariousness with recurring shifts between inferior and superior positions, leader and follower roles. In the first half of the play, the ghosts possessed agency and their movements, diction, and poses suggested confidence and mastery. When the Young Man walked in with a lantern, he was afraid and confused. He is fleeing from Dublin to the West, and does not feel comfortable in county Clare: he feels lost in the darkness, so he is a doubly vulnerable position. The ghosts, however, appeared on the balcony, above both the Young Man and the audience, standing upright, proud, and dignified, speaking in confident, sometimes even arrogant, mocking voices. Their costumes also gave the impression of a once wealthy and proud aristocratic couple who have lost their status through seven centuries of suffering and penance. Unlike the Young

Man, they are not afraid, and wonder about the confusion they see on the Young Man's face: "But what have you to fear?" (*VPl* 764). This makes the Young Man ill-at-ease—which the production represented as fury—as the Young Man is not yet able to act as agent and has to rely on others' help, even though Ireland is his home. He exclaimed with despise and disappointment: "[...] but you are in the right, / I should not be afraid in County Clare; / And should be, or should not be, have no choice, I have to put myself into your hands" (*VPl* 764).

The ghosts then descended and began moving around the Young Man to (intensifying) drumbeats, which appeared like an initiation ritual. This sequence ended suddenly with the Stranger's proposal, "I will put you safe" (*VPl* 765), which marked his initial position of mastery. Soon after this emphatic moment, the Stranger cried out in ecstasy and burst into laughter, crawling around the Young Man not with an air of humbleness or subjugation, but superiority, mockery, excess, and even eroticism, which visibly increased the Young Man's unease and fury. The play text does not give specific directions for movement or laughter at this point in the play, so this production choice clearly emphasized the ghosts' initial agency and deceitful attitude as opposed to the lost, angry, and confused Young Man, terrified of the sounds, the darkness, and his lack of control over events.

Figure 2. Photo credit: Emilia Lloret

The three characters then began marching in formation led by Diarmuid (with the Young Man in between the two ghosts), all emulating Diarmuid's movements. In the performance space, arranged to evoke Yeats's concept of the gyre, the audience was seated very close to the performers – particularly those playing the ghosts. As the trio marched, the gyre pattern represented the pathway up the hill. Lustyik wrote a beautiful "Marching song" for this long scene—a name chosen deliberately over "Travel song" by the composer and director, in order to evoke connotations of warfare. The marching was strangely juxtaposed with the beauty of the melody.

This marching scene showed changes of agency as well: first, Diarmuid was in a position of mastery, but then the Young Man took his place with movements that evoked the master characters of the *commedia dell'arte*, another significant influence on Yeats. The Young Man's place was then taken by Dervorgilla, and before they reached the summit, Diarmuid took back the lead position. Thanks to the use of physical theater, the performers enacting the two ghosts often moved very close to audience members, looking into their eyes; in this way physical theater allowed these liminal characters to affect audiences more intensely and emotionally.

However, after the marching scene but before reaching the summit where the ghosts beg for the Young Man's forgiveness, they began losing confidence and mastery. Their movements became increasingly fragmented and broken,

Figure 3. Photo credit: Emilia Lloret

their facial expressions more desperate, and their diction more sentimental—shaky and close to crying. This helped draw attention to the corporeal and psychic effects of social exclusion and precarity. Unlike the beginning, whenever the ghosts moved their motions were narrated by the Young Man, indicating that they had no agency over their actions and fate. No matter how hard they tried, their visibility and story were dependent on the Young Man's words.

Diarmuid and Dervorgilla also exchange leader and follower roles during the play. This production made it more visible; in the first half of the show, Dervorgilla was silent and only Diarmuid spoke, while Dervorgilla had to imitate his movements and maintain her presence even when she was not doing or saying anything. This arrangement was not only difficult for the performer but also made her body more vulnerable and doubly precarious: as a woman and as a person stigmatized for betraying the nation. In the second half of the play, Dervorgilla took over the agent role from Diarmuid, and continued telling their story to the Young Man with passion and vigor. Yeats deliberately made the lines of Diarmuid and Dervorgilla interchangeable and thought that Dervorgilla might as well be played by a man. As Yeats explains in his notes to *The Dreaming of the Bones*: "Devorgilla's few lines can be given, if need be, to Dermot, and Dervorgilla's part taken by a dancer who has the training of a dancer alone; nor need that masked dancer be a woman" (*VPl* 777). This interchangeability was reinforced by the ghosts' movements in the production, as they exchanged leader and follower positions and their costumes, hairstyles, and masks looked very similar, thus signaling the equality and fluidity between the two characters. The lines assigned to the ghosts are not gendered and do not include any reference which would make the interchangeability of the roles impossible.

The second half of the play is also full of the Young Man's expressions of loathing and rage at the English and the traitors of the Irish nation, and his bitterness and aggression stands in stark contrast with the tenderness and despair with which the ghosts gradually recount their story. Diarmuid and Dervorgilla try to create visibility for themselves, and thanks to the power of dance, gestures, and storytelling, they almost succeed in convincing the Stranger, who, however, refuses to be influenced emotionally: "O, never, never / Shall Diarmuid and Dervorgilla be forgiven. / You have told your story well, so well indeed / I could not help but fall into the mood / And for a while believe that it was true, / Or half believe; but better push on now." (*VPl* 773)

It is important that Yeats wrote a play which gave this potential visibility only to the Stranger and the Young Girl through a combination of dance, movement, gesture, and masks—all of which contributed to the act of storytelling and made their story more powerful and convincing. In contrast, the Young Man wore no mask, moved very little in the space, did not dance, and stood almost motionless throughout the show, using only words to justify his story. The only time he moved more in the space was when Diarmuid and Dervorgilla offered to help him and guide him—a gesture which, however, remained unrequited, as he was not willing to perform a similar act of inclusion for the ghosts.

This dissonance between the Young Man's and the ghosts' stage presence also helped to visualize the contrast between two playing styles: the naturalistic theatrical tradition represented by the Young Man and the new, more powerful, anti-naturalistic way of theater-making embodied by the two ghosts. This reading of Yeats interrogates the naturalistic style of drama which usually works with fixed notions of identity and classifications, while anti-naturalistic theater operates with more fluid notions of identity and refuses traditional categorizations. The Young Man gets anxious when he loses control once again and cannot understand what is going on, as he finds emotions and passion unnatural: "Why do you dance? / Why do you gaze, and with so passionate eyes, / One on the other; and then turn away, / Covering your eyes, and weave it in a dance? / Who are you? what are you? you are not natural" (*VPl* 774). The Young Man describes this dance scene as strange and sweet, but he deliberately refuses strangeness (the other) and sweetness (sentimentality and passion). For him, these ghosts' precarious bodies are sinful and shameful and thus not worthy of sympathy or grief. Yet in the final monologue, the Young Man's language becomes very poetic and moves closer to the ghosts' playing style, as if Yeats was making up for what had been denied from the Young Man's character before.

The second half of the play is also marked by the Young Man shouting "O, never, never / Shall Diarmuid and Dervorgilla be forgiven" (*VPl* 773) three times: two times before they reach the summit and once again at the very end, during the dance, when he already knows he is talking to Diarmuid and Dervorgilla. Three is a magic number in Yeats's works and *The Dreaming of the Bones* illustrates this beautifully: there are three singers, three main characters, three circles around the stage, and Dervorgilla says "being accursed" (*VPl* 770) three times. The Young Man's three exclamations of "O, never, never / Shall Diarmuid and Dervorgilla be forgiven" seem to work as answers and verbal reinforcements of Dervorgilla's three exclamations of "being accursed," which come right before the Young Man's rejections. In all three cases, the power and invisible violence of his words visibly crushed the lovers, and their bodies collapsed, their movements became much more fragmented, and they groan as if they had been murdered. The lovers' body language illustrated that they perceived the Young Man's words as an oppressive performative speech directed at them, which affected the way they behaved, identifying more and more with the subjugated, inferior position that the Young Man's words assigned to people like Diarmuid and Dervorgilla.

Cry-Cooke's visceral choreography fluctuated between a mix of confident, erotic, and fragile movements, at times bursting into ecstasy, suggesting the lovers' wish to be liberated from their punishment, societal constraints, and judgments. The movements of the performers conveyed the strenuousness of their predicament and the punishment they had to perform in hope of liberation. The performers playing the ghosts moved mostly on the ground and, even when standing, seemed bent and broken, except for their first appearance. The Young Man never crouched or crawled during the production, and his body language did not convey as much physical discomfort as that of the ghosts, apart from his fear of being lost, and his confusion regarding the ghosts' identities. In other words, he never let himself be blown away fully by the power of desire and refused the needs of the body in order to stay true to his nationalistic ideals. The Young Man's expressions of refusal also put the ghosts in a physiologically vulnerable position right before the decisive dance scene which determined their fate: they had to dance knowing that they danced only to receive the final and most powerful refusal.

Another interesting aspect of the production was the reinforcement of *The Dreaming of the Bones*'s bird motif through costumes, masks, and choreography. The text recurrently signals the connection between the lonely birds and the ghosts: "Somewhere among great rocks on the scarce grass / Birds cry, they cry their loneliness" (*VPl* 763). The Young Girl describes their story with a similar image: "They have not that luck, / But are more lonely" (*VPl* 769), "[t]hese are alone, / Being accursed" (*VPl* 770). Lustyik's music deliberately imitated bird songs, a theme that was supported by Cry-Cooke's choreography and Yvette Picque's costumes and masks. Both the chorus (the three musicians) and the ghosts conveyed fragile, fluid, bird-like movements with their arms and heads, while the costumes included half-masks whose noses were reminiscent of beaks and the performers' hair was styled to give an earthy, disheveled impression. During rehearsals, mask-work was incorporated into exercises for physicalizing character whereby actors chose a line that represented the essence of the character's mood and worked it into a piece of clay. Cry-Cooke's choice was the phrase "I will not answer for the dead" (*VPl* 765), and his mask-work was directly informed by the image of a bird of prey swirling above Diarmuid's head. He carved a big swirl to the left side and created a protruding nose for the mask which reflected his pride, but also his sense of guilt and his fear of being attacked from above. This choice dialogued nicely with the play text which recurrently hints at the ghosts' fear of remaining lonely like the birds, which whirl above their heads and cry out their shared loneliness. This mixture of pride, guilt, and fear in Diarmuid's character was also manifested in the shifts between master and subjugated positions his movements and body language conveyed onstage.

Costuming choices also highlighted Diarmuid and Dervorgilla's relationship with one another and with the land itself. The ghosts' clothes, just like those of the three musicians, were a greyish brown earthy color, marked by white stains from the chalk powder poured all over the ground. This created the impression that the characters belonged to the landscape of the Burren, and that they were more at home there than the Young Man, yet their visibility was denied by their fellow Irishman. It was also remarkable that the ghosts' hands and bodies were close throughout the production but never touched. This element of the choreography highlights that the play speaks more broadly to those people who, for some reason, are not allowed to express their love, who cannot kiss or hold hands in public without being judged and condemned by society, and who are forced to feel ashamed of their story and desires: "but when he has bent his head / Close to her head, or hand would slip in hand, / The memory of their crime flows up between / And drives them apart" (*VPl* 772). They have to perform a "strange penance" (*VPL* 771), as "[t]hough eyes can meet, their lips can never meet" (*VPl* 771), and as the Young Girl laments "nor any pang / That is so bitter as that double glance, / Being accursed" (VPl 771). The reason this double glance is so bitter is that anytime their eyes meet, it reminds them of the impossibility of their love; the moment they establish intimacy through their glance, it is immediately broken by the very knowledge of its impossibility. The Young Man also denies the reality of their desire by claiming that "when lips meet / And have not living nerves, it is no meeting" (*VPl* 771). With this claim he also tries to justify why his forgiveness would be unnecessary and wrong, refusing to recognize their desires and feelings as valid and worthy of inclusion in the master-narrative.

DancePlayers' take on Yeats's play made more visible the play's interrogation of the validity of not only naturalistic theater but also political narrow-mindedness, which operates using a discourse of hatred and obsession with enemies of the nation, expecting people to put aside emotions and love when it comes to the national cause. While the Young Man speaks to the centuries of oppression the Irish endured under colonial rule, he too is in a vulnerable position, fleeing from police alone in the darkness. Yet, though oppressed himself, his reaction is to oppress. Although his attitude is anti-imperialist, his treatment of Diarmuid and Dervorgilla brings him closer to a totalizing and oppressive imperialist ethic that idealizes principles of duty and sacrifice. DancePlayers' *The Dreaming of the Bones* illustrated, through the power of physical theater techniques, that the play is more sympathetic to the two outcast lovers whose bodies can no longer touch and whose desires remain unfulfilled. Even though forgiveness is denied, this dramaturgical decision has a more emphatic emotional influence on the audience. It points at the cruelty and absurdity of the rigid, oppressive socio-political institutions that the Young Man represents, and which he justifies with references to Ireland's painful colonial past: "Our country, if that crime were uncommitted, / Had been most beautiful" (*VPl* 774). The Young Man also stands for the mythology of sacrificial martyrdom and republican rhetoric which, as Susan Harris explained in *Gender and Modern Irish Drama*, works "as a normative force" designed to exclude and erase those who do not adhere to any totalizing vision of heroic nationalist resistance. As Harris further noted, Yeats established the foundation of this sacrificial tradition with early works such as *Cathleen ni Houlihan* or *The Countess Cathleen*, but later revolted against the idea; *The Dreaming of the Bones* serves as a spectacular example of this change.

By allowing both the Young Man and the lovers to tell their stories, *The Dreaming of the Bones* offers interweaving narratives, poses difficult questions about what and who can be included in the concept of Irishness, and most importantly, refuses to impose a single, totalizing narrative on the audience. In Adrian Frazier's words, the aim is "to cross the national narrative with counternarratives, not of nations, but of genders, sexualities, localities, and congeries of extranational interests." DancePlayers' mission to apply physical theater to Yeats's plays can indeed bring them closer to contemporary audiences, highlighting how ably Yeats's drama speaks to the present by addressing the still complex relationship between nationalism, sexual desire, alterity and the body.

NOTES

1. Helen Meany, "Physical theatre comes to town," *The Irish Times* (January 9, 1997).
2. Claudia Kinahan, "Irish Bodies: The Rise of Dance Theatre," *TN2 Magazine* (April 6, 2017).
3. Adrian Frazier, "Queering the Irish Renaissance: The Masculinities of Moore, Martyn, and Yeats," in *Gender and Sexualities in Modern Ireland*, eds. Anthony Bradley and Maryann Gialanella Valiulis (Amherst: University of Massachusetts Press, 1997), 8–39: 10.
4. Nicholas Grene, *The Politics of Irish Drama: Plays in Context from Boucicault to Friel* (Cambridge and New York: Cambridge University Press, 1999), 86.
5. Kinahan, "Irish Bodies."
6. Kinahan, "Irish Bodies."
7. For a detailed discussion of precarity and physical theater see Marissia Fragkou, *Ecologies of Precarity in Twenty-First Century Theatre: Politics, Affect, Responsibility* (London and New York: Methuen Drama, 2019).
8. Frazier, "Queering the Irish Renaissance," 11.
9. Susan Cannon Harris, *Gender and Modern Irish Drama* (Bloomington: Indiana University Press, 2002), 10.
10. Harris, *Gender and Modern Irish Drama*, 10.
11. Frazier, "Queering the Irish Renaissance," 10.
12. For more information about the show, contact DancePlayers Company directly at danceplayers company@gmail.com.

Notes on Contributors

CHARLES I. ARMSTRONG is a professor of English literature at the University of Agder, in Norway. He is the Vice President of the International Yeats Society and a co-director of the Yeats International Summer School, as well as the president of the Nordic Association of English Studies. He is the author of three monographs, including *Reframing Yeats: Genre, Allusion and History* (Bloomsbury, 2013). He has co-edited five volumes of essays, the most recent of which is *Terrorizing Images: Trauma and Ekphrasis in Contemporary Literature* (De Gruyter, 2020).

ZSUZSANNA BALÁZS is an Irish Research Council Postgraduate Scholar in the O'Donoghue Centre for Drama, Theatre and Performance at the National University of Ireland, Galway. She completed her BA in Romance Philology (specialized in Italian Studies) and her MA in English Studies (specialized in Postcolonial Literatures) at Pázmány Péter Catholic University in Budapest. Her PhD research explores the dynamics between the queer and the normative in W. B. Yeats's and Gabriele D'Annunzio's drama, focusing on unorthodox representations of gender, power, and desire in light of the playwrights' queer and feminist networks.

INÉS BIGOT is a fourth-year doctoral student working under the supervision of Alexandra Poulain at the University of Sorbonne Nouvelle. Her current research focuses on the poetics and the politics of the dancing body in the plays of W. B. Yeats and Wole Soyinka, a topic to which she has devoted several articles. She looks at the dissident potential of dance which is simultaneously staged as the untamable opposite of language and as a subversive discourse in the plays of the Irish and Nigerian playwrights. Her research is nourished by her own experience as a dancer: she practiced ballet for ten years in a conservatory before adopting a more theoretical approach to the art of dancing.

MARGARET MILLS HARPER is Glucksman Professor of Contemporary Writing in English at the University of Limerick, Ireland. She has published two monographs, including *Wisdom of Two: The Spiritual and Literary Collaboration of George and W. B. Yeats* (Oxford UP, 2006). Her scholarly editions comprise two volumes of *Yeats's "Vision" Papers* (Macmillan 1992 and 2001, co-edited with Robert Anthony Martinich and George Mills Harper) and both the 1925 and 1937 versions of W. B. Yeats's *A Vision* (Scribner, co-edited with Catherine E. Paul, 2008 and 2015). She served as director of the Yeats International Summer School from 2013 to 2015 and as the first President of the International Yeats Society.

LLOYD (MEADHBH) HOUSTON is Hertford College–Faculty of English DPhil Scholar in Irish Literature in English at the University of Oxford. Their thesis explores Irish modernism and the politics of sexual health. Other research interests include literature and obscenity, queer modernisms, and the social history of medicine. Their work has appeared in the *Review of English Studies*, the *Irish Studies Review*, and the *Times Literary Supplement*.

AKIKO MANABE is Professor of English at Shiga University, Japan. She specializes in American and Irish Modernist poetry and drama. She has recently focused on the Japanese influence on European and American modernism, especially with relation to *Noh* and *kyogen*. Recent publications include the co-authored book *Hemingway and Ezra Pound in Venezia* (2015); and articles on Yeats, Pound, Hemingway, and Hearn in *Études Anglaises* (2015), *Japanese Artists and Modernism in Europe and America* (2016), *Cultural Hybrids of (Post)Modernism: Japanese/Western Literature, Art and Philosophy* (co-editor, 2016), *Overview of Modernism* (2017), *Encounter of Texts: Heritage and Influence of Brontë Sisters* (2019), and *Yeats and Asia* (2020). Since 2017 she has produced a series of performances of new *kyogen* based on the work of Yeats and Hearn in Ireland and Japan.

CLAIRE NALLY is Associate Professor of Modern and Contemporary Literature at Northumbria University, UK. She researches Irish Studies, Neo-Victorianism, Gender, and Subcultures. She published her first monograph, *Envisioning Ireland: W. B. Yeats's Occult Nationalism* (2009), followed by her second book, *Selling Ireland: Advertising, Literature and Irish Print Culture 1891–1922* (written with John Strachan). She has co-edited a volume on Yeats and two volumes on gender, as well as the library series *Gender and Popular Culture* for Bloomsbury (with Angela Smith).

ALEXANDRA POULAIN is Professor of postcolonial literature and theatre at the University of Sorbonne Nouvelle (France). She has published widely on modern and contemporary Irish drama and performance, with a special focus on Yeats and Beckett. Her latest book *Irish Drama, Modernity and the Passion Play* (Palgrave, 2016) looks at rewritings of the Passion narrative as a modality of political resistance in Irish plays from Synge to the present day. Her current research focuses on decolonial projects in contemporary art. She is the current President of the International Yeats Society.

MARIA RITA DRUMOND VIANA is a lecturer and researcher in the Department of Foreign Languages and Literatures at the Universidade Federal de Santa Catarina (UFSC) in Brazil, where she works on life writing, Irish Studies, and translation. Her thesis on W. B. Yeats's use of public letters to editors in nineteenth-century periodicals was defended in 2015. During 2019 she was on an academic sabbatical at the University of Toronto to conduct research on Virginia Woolf as part of a larger project on writers' correspondences.